P9-AON-139

QUEST FOR THE SOUL

*Our Search
for Deeper Meaning*

Dr. Robert L. Wise

A
JANET
THOMA
BOOK

THOMAS NELSON PUBLISHERS
Nashville • Atlanta • London • Vancouver

Copyright © 1996 by Robert L. Wise

All rights reserved. Written permission must be secured from the publisher to use or reproduce any part of this book, except for brief quotations in critical reviews or articles.

Published in Nashville, Tennessee, by Thomas Nelson, Inc., Publishers, and distributed in Canada by Word Communications, Ltd., Richmond, British Columbia.

The Bible version used in this publication is THE NEW KING JAMES VERSION. Copyright © 1979, 1980, 1982, 1990 Thomas Nelson, Inc., Publishers.

Scripture quotations noted NIV are taken from the HOLY BIBLE, NEW INTERNATIONAL VERSION®. Copyright © 1973, 1978, 1984 by International Bible Society. Used by permission of Zondervan Bible Publishing House. All rights reserved.

Every effort was made to secure permission for all material which may require permission. Those having information regarding permission should contact the publisher so that changes can be made to subsequent printings.

Excerpts from "Are Music and Movies Killing America's Soul?" 6/12/95, credit © 1995 TIME Inc. Reprinted by permission.

Seventeen words from *The Cloud of Unknowing,* translated by Clifton Wolters, (Penguin Classics, 1961), copyright © Clifton Wolters, 1961.

"Dear Joanna" from *Living by the Word: Selected Writings 1973–1987,* copyright © 1988 by Alice Walker, reprinted by permission of Harcourt Brace & Company.

From *Soul Food* by Sheila Ferguson, copyright © 1989 by Sheila Ferguson, Used by permission of Grove/Atlantic, Inc.

Library of Congress Cataloging-in-Publication Data

Wise, Robert L.
    Quest for the soul : humanity's loss, pursuit, and spiritual recovery of the thumbprint of God / Robert L. Wise.
      p. cm.
    Includes bibliographical references.
    ISBN 0-7852-7554-1 (pbk.)
    1. Soul. 2. Soul—Quotations, maxims, etc. 3. Spiritual life—Christianity. 4. Wise, Robert L. I. Title.
BT741.2.W57 1996
233'.5—dc20   95–49638
                                                CIP

Printed in the United States of America.
1 2 3 4 5 6 — 00 99 98 97 96

To the Brantley family,
a people of soul,
and
to the memory of Margueritte Jo,
mother, wife, companion, and example

CONTENTS

About the Author

Robert L. Wise, Ph.D., is rector of The Church of the Redeemer in Oklahoma City, Oklahoma, and author or co-author of fifteen books, including *Windows of the Soul, All That Remains,* and *The Dawning.* Dr. Wise is the principal lecturer for the Bethel series in Canada, Germany, and the United States.

Acknowledgments

This book would not have been possible without the diligent and relentless research of Joanie Brantley. Her thoughtful reading, editing, and probing of many a library shelf made these pages happen. In a fundamental sense, Joanie is the coauthor of this work.

I am also indebted to Dr. Larry Correa for his help with computer problems and to his daughter Jamie for her assistance. I owe Paul Cardin a special word of appreciation for his help in compiling the texts. And, as has been true for so many past books, Janet Thoma remains the finest guide and editor a writer can have.

Robert L. Wise
Holy Cross Day
September 14, 1995

PART ONE

Disconnecting:
The Loss of the Soul

Chapter 1

THE
JOURNEY
BEGINS

Once upon a time I lost my soul.

No horrendous sins or exotic misadventures wait in the wings for an airing. My story doesn't have any salacious twists or tales of debauchery and depravity. Mephistopheles didn't appear one midnight offering immortality in exchange for my heart's desire. Actually, spiritual pursuits and church work demanded most of my time.

The busy life of running a church, being a husband, being a father to four children, trying to pay bills without enough money, writing books, and intending to do good simply took its toll. I lost touch with the center of my being. My soul just disappeared beneath the weight of college degrees, sacks of groceries, piles of bills, and the burden of too many worries and not enough hours in the day for extended prayer, personal reflection, and solace. It withered from neglect. Strangely, I didn't even notice the loss for a long time. Mistaking busyness for meaning, activity for purpose, the sheer inertia of preoccupation with good things kept me from an awareness of having lost contact with the best thing. Sixty-hour work weeks have a way of blurring one's vision.

Discovering the Zombies

I remember a growing awareness of being surrounded by multitudes of other lost souls. I saw their images in nearly every movie I attended (and I saw at least one a week). Antiheroes had become the new heroes; degenerate people with degrading values gained cinema star status. Gangsters, psychotics, and the promiscuous were Hollywood's fascination. The music industry bestowed on us rappers, Madonna, Mick Jagger, and a host of rock stars (many of whom jettisoned themselves into eternity with drugs) for our adulation. Something was seriously amiss.

Clergy offered me the first clues about my own loss. While many were the finest people in the world, some of my colleagues operated with ambition to shame a politician. Many professional religionists preached about the problems of the multitudes but were indifferent to the pain of individuals. Others operated the local church with the same spiritual concern the branch management of Sears uses in selling tires. Soul was definitely missing.

Churches attempt to replace soul with "something." In the 1960s, the theological enterprise became serious about the business of creating God in our own image. Theologians poured theology into sociological molds. Correct belief was out; nervous activism was in. Much of the subsequent social action was without soul. At the other end of the spectrum, evangelism often was not helping people recover their souls as much as changing their intellectual outlook by creating an emotional moment of decision "for Jesus." Rather than the soul being filled with the indwelling Christ, the end product was signing up for church membership. At the time I didn't understand what I was seeing, but I recognized the vain and empty terrain, the wasteland of T. S. Eliot's hollow men.

Looking for the Treasure in the Field

My problem first manifested itself as a hunger, emptiness, haunting inner loneliness I couldn't fill through any relationship. Like so many people, I really didn't know how to practice the faith I believed in.

One afternoon I collapsed across my desk exhausted. Several years before I had started this new congregation with 5 people. In short order the 5 became 150 and soon turned into 500. The denomination lauded me around the country, promoting me as one to share my success with the struggling. I had become something akin to God's golden boy.

And now I was exhausted.

To gain the world and lose one's soul is one thing. Building a suburban church and losing your psyche was quite another. I was impoverished and in deep need of respite. More important, I knew I was another of Eliot's spiritual scarecrows. I needed help.

A quick look back over my studies revealed that I had spent a great deal of energy studying emotions and how psychotherapy worked. I didn't need more insight into the mind. Another Greek exegetical study of the Bible wasn't the answer either. Reading the latest novel or a new book on the latest advances in theology couldn't satisfy. I needed instructors capable of teaching me about the soul and helping me find it.

The journey proved to be difficult because few people knew what I was talking about. Protestant seminaries were of no help. Places of intellectual combat, they seldom offer much nurture. Most of my colleagues found my questions interesting but mystifying. And then I accidentally (on God's purpose) stumbled across the Benedictine Monastery at Pecos, New Mexico.

The Pecos religious community of men and women devoted themselves to the pursuit of the soul through study of the Scriptures, contemplation, worship, and the insights of depth psychology. They were eager to share their paths through the detours set up by the modern world. I took a sabbatical, moved into the monastery, and began the rigorous spiritual life starting every day with community morning prayer at six o'clock. The ensuing weeks proved to be the most valuable of my life. During meditation, I found stepping stones. Hidden trails appeared in Scripture. I recovered secret spiritual lagoons and cool grottoes of prayer discovered by ancient saints. Each place was a new soul center.

The Benedictines taught me to interpret my dreams as a means of spiritual direction. The insights of depth psychology aided this profound method of spiritual "questing." To my amazement, dream tools proved to be one of the most significant aids in finding my displaced soul. Peace and tranquility returned to my life in these gentle surroundings of amazing serenity. I had recovered my soul.

In the following pages, I offer you not a road map so much as voices. As I made my pilgrimage, the calls of these saints, friends, and sojourners kept me on track and helped me hear again the sounds of eternity. The excerpts from their writings aren't offered as a quick read but for slow and careful contemplation.

Finding yourself is not an inward trek like peeling away the sections of an onion until you hit some secret inner essence. Rather, you are looking for the fingerprint of God in your life. The task is to follow the direction and advice of those who already know the inner way well.

The need is for centering. While pursuing an art degree, I studied ceramics. Throwing pots on a wheel proved to be one of the most exhilarating experiences of my life. I became so addicted to the wonderful feel of wet clay oozing between my fingers that time would lose all meaning. I was learning that the secret of working the potter's wheel is the same as finding one's soul.

In *Centering*, Mary Caroline Richards's marvelous little book on poetry, pottery, and personhood, she writes, "As human beings functioning as potters, we center ourselves and our clay. And we all know how necessary it is to be 'on center' ourselves if we wish to bring our clay 'into center' and not merely to agitate it or bully it. As organisms in the natural rhythms of birth, growth, and death, we experience metamorphosis throughout our lives, as our bodies grow and change from infancy to ripeness, as our capacities for inner experience enlarge and strengthen."[1] Centering is our all important clue.

The wheel is spinning, and the time has come. Transformation is waiting in the wings. Let's see if we can find our way to the center of your universe.

Chapter 2

INTO THE
VOID

We need to know something is missing before we can go looking for "it." Until people realize they have misplaced their souls, religious talk doesn't connect on a significant level.

Loss of soul takes on many shapes and sizes.

On April 20, 1995, the day after the terrorist bombing in Oklahoma City, Joe Davis discovered his baseball coach was killed in the Alfred P. Murrah Federal Building. The day of the funeral Joe's mother brought the twelve-year-old to talk with me. Because I was his pastor, Joe thought I could tell him why someone would blow up a building, killing 169 people, injuring over 300 people, orphaning 30 children and leaving 219 others with only 1 parent.

Everyone living through these terrible and traumatic times has asked Joe's question many times. Why do human beings inflict such pain on each other? Could the loss of soul be the answer?

Talking with Joe, I became aware of a new aspect of the tragedies filling the history of the twentieth century. We have become accustomed to explaining all deviant behavior in psychological categories: bombers, murderers, thieves, and rapists are labeled psychopaths, sociopaths, psychotics, and character disorder cases. But do any of these diagnoses answer Joe's questions? No. Perhaps, contemporary psychology missed the most important category of all. Loss of soul.

Is it possible that sane people are capable of horrible deeds of malice and abuse? Can people lose their perspectives so completely that with total indifference they badly hurt others? The answer is painfully obvious.

While soul loss is gradual and a matter of degree, dissipation produces disconnection with God, others, and oneself. Perspective goes askew and consequences are clouded. Actions no longer have meaning. Behavior is self-indulgent. Rational people do very irrational things.

Christians *must* be able to make contact with the void in society and speak to the emptiness. Unless Christian people can understand the signs of the illness, their remedy of faith will never be used.

Loss of soul takes many forms: banality . . . materialism . . . duplicity . . . meaninglessness . . . emptiness . . . indifference. Here are some of the sounds, conversations, reflections, and indicators of what forfeiture of soul looks like. These readings are a collection of word pictures depicting the crisis. They offer mirrors to help us see ourselves in the light of others' experiences.

Consider these examples well. They are the symptoms of a serious disease.

The Way of the World

People are incurably religious creatures. We have now even learned how to invent a religion that doesn't need

God. Hedonism, entertainment, and banality are the new Trinity. Take a look at the new faith offered through television.

Happiness Is
Russell Baker

The Gorths have found happiness through faith in television. "Absolute faith in the doctrine of materialism as revealed on Channels 2, 4, 5, 7, 9, and 20," says Bill, "has made a new person of me."

"Fabulous," says Cora Sue. "Twice as much happiness power as my old faith product."

Bill's conversion began one day when, listless, Vietnam-weary and tired of his marriage, he sat in the evening traffic jam slouched at the wheel of his Hupmobile. "Suddenly," he says, "I realized that it wasn't happening. When I got home that night I told Cora Sue, 'We've got to find something that will make it happen.' That night Channel 4 spoke to me for the first time. 'Rhinoceros makes it happen,' Channel 4 said." . . .

Seeing Bill's new happiness, Cora Sue began taking instructions from Channel 9. One night after Bill had hitched his Rhinoceros at the curb and fought off the beauties swarming to kiss him, he entered the kitchen to find Cora Sue wearing a Queen's crown. That afternoon, on the instruction from Channel 9, she had quit greasing the bread with the high-priced spread and had switched to new improved gummoid margarine.

Since that day both Gorths have become contented, if somewhat hysterical, people. This gives an odd quality to attempts to make conversation with them. Commonplace conversational gambits such as, "Why am I so miserable all the time?" bring answers such as, "It's that old product you're using on your hair, friend."

"Fabulous," says Cora Sue. "Twice as much anti-misery power, too."

Like so many converts, the Gorths have no patience with skeptics. "What! Not believe in the new washday miracle?" Bill will ask, "Why, man, you might as well deny the existence of twice as much anti-perspirant power. You might as well say there is no crunchy goodness flavor packed into every wholesome kernel of springtime freshness."

Nothing irritates Bill Gorth more than someone pointing out that he talks like a fool. "Of course I talk like a fool," he says. "Cora Sue and I both talk like fools. It is our way of being absolutely loyal to our beliefs. Look, this whole neighborhood, this whole city, this whole country is swarming with people who practice the same faith as we do. The only difference is that they're ashamed of it. It conceals their shame if they can laugh at the language of the channels, but it doesn't stop them from living by the message. Cora Sue and I believe in being perfectly honest about our faith."

"Fabulous," says Cora Sue. "Twice as much fool-exposure power, too."

Happiness to Bill and Cora Sue is belief in faster starting, brighter laundry, quicker relief, fresher smoke, longer protection, shinier floors, crunchier goodness, crisper chips, sexier lips, slimmer hips, and happier trips.

"As a religion," says Bill, "I'll admit it's not much, but at least it is suited to today's world."

"Fabulous," says Cora Sue. "Twice as much fun as that old moralizing, too."

from *Soundings,*
edited by Robert A. Raines, p. 76.

What church does not hear a steady diet of preaching warning of the seduction of "things." Yet, American society has a singular devotion to materialism, the worship of prosperity, status, and the accumulation of things. Consider whether worship of success is answer or an illness.

The Goddess of Success
Norman Pophopete

Blessed are the meek, for they shall inherit the earth.

Let me introduce myself. I am a man who at the precocious age of thirty-five experienced an astonishing revelation: it is better to be a success than a failure. Having been penetrated by this great truth concerning the nature of things, my mind was now open for the first time to a series of corollary perceptions, each one as dizzying in its impact as the Original revelation itself. Money, I now saw (no one, of course, had ever seen it before), was important: it was better to be rich than to be poor. Power, I now saw (moving on to higher subtleties), was desirable: it was better to give orders than to take them. Fame, I now saw (how courageous of me not to flinch), was unqualifiedly delicious: it was better to be recognized than to be anonymous.

This book represents an effort to explain why it should have taken someone like myself so long to arrive at such apparently elementary discoveries. . . .

My second purpose in telling the story of my own career is to provide a concrete setting for a diagnosis of the curiously contradictory feelings our culture instills in us toward the ambition for success, and toward each of its various goals: money, power, fame, and social position. On the one hand, we are commanded to become successful—that is, to acquire more of these worldly goods than we began with, and to do so by our own exertions; on the other hand, it is impressed upon us by means both direct and devious that if we obey the commandment, we shall find ourselves falling victim to the radical corruption of the spirit which, given the nature of what is nowadays called the "system," the pursuit of success requires and which its attainment always bespeaks. On the one hand, "the exclusive worship of the @!*#!-goddess SUCCESS," as William James put it in a famous remark, "is our national disease"; on the other hand, a contempt for success is the consensus of the national literature for the past hundred years and more. On the one hand, our culture teaches us to shape our lives in accordance with the hunger for worldly things; on the other hand, it spitefully contrives to make us ashamed of the presence of those hungers in ourselves and to deprive us as far as possible of any pleasure in their satisfaction.

Nothing, I believe, defines the spiritual character of American life more saliently than this contradiction, and I doubt that many Americans, whether they be successes or failures in their careers, can have escaped its consequences. . . .

For taking my career as seriously as I do in this book, I will no doubt be accused of self-inflation and therefore of tastelessness. So be it. There was a time when to talk candidly about sex was similarly regarded as tasteless—a betrayal of what D. H. Lawrence once called "the dirty little secret." For many of us, of course, this is no longer the case. But judging by the embarrassment that a frank discussion of one's feelings about one's own success, or the lack of it, invariably causes in polite company today, ambition (itself a species of lustful hunger) seems to be replacing erotic lust as the prime dirty little secret of the well-educated American soul.

from *Soundings,*
edited by Robert A. Raines, p. 129.

Where do people turn when they've lost their soul? Where do they look for warmth and understanding? Consider where people gravitate for a touch of care . . . even if artificial.

The Brass Rail Communion Table
Gay Talese, novelist

It was the sort of West Side bar that even a libel lawyer would call a "dive." The stools were patched, the neon light was cracked, the drinkers seemed tired, dusty and lonely— like the neighborhood. And yet the blonde girl behind the bar did not fit the scene at all. She possessed a just-bathed look and was obviously intelligent and very polite and cheerful. When the other barmaids would steal her tips, she would not complain; when one of the men at the bar would become insulting, she would seem not to hear.

The owner of the bar could never understand why she had applied in June for employment in such a place. He did not know . . . that she was a University of California graduate in sociology, and that the $50 a week summer job behind the bar was part of her "course" in the study of the drinker, the decadent neighborhood, and its effect upon loneliness.

He was not upset, just dumbfounded when Astrid Huerter told him this. And he was astonished too, when she said the employment there had been "very educational." Later Miss Huerter, a twenty-one-year-old native of Germany who got a scholarship to study in this country, said that many of her preconceived notions of life in a dive had proved to be false. There is a kind of "morality" to be found there, she said, and many of the regular drinkers, some of them derelicts, soon began to worry about her, to wonder what "a nice girl like you" is doing in such a place.

"A few of them said they knew of other jobs for me that weren't so 'low class,'" she said. "They wanted to rescue me—they who could barely help themselves." Most of the regular patrons, she said, came to the bar not out of a need to drink or to pass the time of night; they came rather "out of a desperate need to communicate with someone and a desire to be heard." If it was merely alcohol that they wanted, they could have got it at half the price from a liquor store; and if they wished merely to pass time, they could have gone to the movies. . . . But only in the neighborhood bar could they be certain of being heard and that was her job there—professional listener. . . . "In New York . . . people do not have time to listen. Here everything is 'getting ahead' and 'progress'—and 'money.' Here you have to pay people to listen. And that is what a barmaid does."

from Creative Brooding,
edited by Robert A. Raines, p. 23.

And what becomes of us when we simply accept the loss of soul? What do we become when we give up on the possibility of genuine spirituality? Consider Camus' answer.

I Have Accepted Duplicity
Albert Camus, author

The idea that comes most naturally to man, as if from his very nature, is the idea of his innocence. . . . Each of us insists on being innocent at all cost, even if he has to accuse the whole human race and heaven itself. You won't delight a man by complimenting him on the efforts by which he has become intelligent or generous. On the other hand, he will beam if you admire his natural generosity. Inversely, if you tell a criminal that his crime is not due to his nature or his character but to unfortunate circumstances, he will be extravagantly grateful to you. . . . It's a matter of dodging judgment. Since it is hard to dodge it, tricky to get one's nature simultaneously admired and excused, they all strive to be rich. Why? Did you ever ask yourself? For power, of course. But especially because wealth shields from immediate judgment, takes you out of the subway crowd to enclose you in a chromium-plated automobile, isolates you in huge protected lawns, Pullmans, first-class cabins. Wealth, cher ami, is not quite acquittal, but reprieve, and that's always worth taking.

Above all, don't believe your friends when they ask you to be sincere with them. They merely hope you will encourage them in the good opinion they have of themselves by providing them with the additional assurance they will find in your promise of sincerity. How could sincerity be a condition of friendship? A liking for truth at any cost is a passion that spares nothing and that nothing resists. It's a vice, at times a comfort, or a selfishness. Therefore, if you are in that situation, don't hesitate: promise to tell the truth and then lie as best to prove your affection.

This is so true that we rarely confide in those who are better than we. Rather, we are more inclined to flee their society. Most often, on the other hand, we confess to those who are like us and who share our weaknesses. Hence we don't want to improve ourselves or be bettered, for we should first have to be judged in default. We merely wish to be pitied and encouraged in the course we have chosen. In short we should like, at the same time, to cease being guilty and yet not to make the effort of cleansing ourselves. Not enough cynicism and not enough virtue. We lack the energy of evil as well as the energy of good . . . however that may be, after prolonged research on myself, I brought out the fundamental duplicity of the human being. Then I realized, as a result of delving into my memory, that modesty helped me to shine, humility to conquer, and virtue to oppress. . . .

And why should I change, since I have found the happiness that suits me? I have accepted duplicity instead of being upset about it.

from *Creative Brooding*,
edited by Robert A. Raines, p. 105.

The Famous

Take a look at the void from the perspective of the famous and the young.

What Do I Care?
Marcello Mastroianni, actor

Question: Are you a socialist yourself?

Answer: I'm the son of workers. What else could I be? I'll admit I'm a rose-water socialist—that is, I'm not active. I don't belong to the party and I avoid involvement, because it means compromise. So I stand in the window and watch. . . .

Question: Many movie marriages wind up on the rocks. Why has yours lasted?

Answer: I've accepted my wife's defects and she's accepted mine. This is out of sufferance and I suppose because we're modern about it. It's useless to try and escape ourselves. Maybe we're not ideal together, but maybe we are. We're both full of defects, many defects. Maybe we weren't made to be together; but for this very reason it might be too easy not to stay together. So we say, "Let's stick it out all the same." It's a kind of game we want to make work.

Question: Does your Catholicism have nothing to do with why you remain married?

Answer: No, I'm not a real Catholic, anyway—even though I am religious. Jesus Christ is an admirable example, but he's too remote from men of today to be a model. Or he's too much of one to be understood and followed. A man who dies for others is moving and admirable, but how many followers can he have in a world filled with people who will hardly help you across the street, let alone die for you?

Question: You believe in a life after death?

Answer: Truthfully, no. If I did, life would be more noble, more interesting, because it would have an ultimate goal—that of continuing. If I were a profound Catholic and believed in the afterlife of the soul, I'd be a man of greater force and more clear-minded, because I'd have a precise purpose to prepare myself for. But since I fear everything will end in death, I say, "What do I care?"

from *Creative Brooding,*
edited by Robert A. Raines, p. 27.

And the Young

Going After Cacciato
Tim O'Brien

The facts, even when beaded on a chain, still did not have a real order. Events did not flow. The facts were separate and haphazard and random even as they happened, episodic, broken, no smooth transitions, no sense of events unfolding from prior events—

The Spirit of Bayonet
Unknown

1 July 1969

Dear Mom and Dad:

In many respects the Army is not as bad as I expected, but overall, it's still the worst thing that ever happened to me. The thing that makes me angriest is the constant harassment for no apparent reason. Actually there is a reason for it, but when you figure it out you wish there weren't one at all—they want us to get angry enough to kill. It works—one fellow I know is a C.O. [conscientious objector] and he gets harassed more than anyone. They give him extra guard duty, trash details, yard details—anything that comes up—just because of his political beliefs.

E got really depressed this afternoon when they issued us our rifles. An M-14 is a pretty useless weapon for hunting or target shooting—the only thing it can be used really effectively and efficaciously for is to kill a human being. I still don't feel like a killer—I guess I will in 3 weeks, but I don't like it. If it were not against the law to express political opinions in this country, I'd tell _____ to go to Canada.

from *Soundings*,
edited by Robert A. Raines, p. 104.

The Rules of Attraction
Brent Easton Ellis

"Peter?"

The table looks up and falls silent.

"I thought my name was Brian," I say, without looking at her.

She laughs, probably high. I can see her hands, her fingernails aren't painted black anymore. It looks like cement color. "Oh well, yeah. How are you?" she asks.

"Eating." I point at the plate. All the guys are looking at her. This is a highly uncomfortable situation.

"You going to the party tonight?" she asks.

"Yeah. I'm going to the party tonight. You going to the party tonight?" Meaningless.

"Yeah." She seemed nervous. The guys are intimidating her. She was actually okay last night, just too drunk. She's probably good in bed. I look over at Tim, who's checking her out. "Yeah, I am."

"Well, I guess I'll see you there." I look at Norris and roll my eyes up.

"Okay," she says, lingering, looking around the room.

"Okay, see you there, bye," I mutter. "God."

"Okay, well," she coughs. "See you."

"Go away," I say under my breath.

from *The Rules of Attraction*, pp. 48–49.

Taking a Hard Second Look

Nothing exposes the *void* like suffering, death, and disillusionment. The personal discovery of duplicity, deceptiveness, and limitation can scatter the facades we live behind . . . and the emptiness they mask.

Consider. What if you picked up today's paper and discovered your obituary was on the funeral page? What would it say?

Reading Your Own Obituary
Nicholas Halasz, author

One morning in 1888, Nobel, inventor of dynamite, the man who had spent his life amassing a fortune from the manufacture and sale of weapons of destruction, awoke to read his own obituary. The obituary was printed as a result of a simple journalistic error—Alfred's brother had died, and a French reporter carelessly reported the death of the wrong brother. Any man would be disturbed under the circumstances, but to Alfred Nobel the shock was overwhelming. He saw himself as the world saw him—"the dynamite king," the great industrialist who had made an immense fortune from explosives. This—as far as the general public was concerned—was the entire purpose of his life. None of his true intentions—to break down the barriers that separated men and ideas—were recognized or given serious consideration. He was quite simply a merchant of death, and for that alone would he be remembered. . . . As he read his obituary with horror, Nobel resolved to make clear to the world the true meaning and purpose of his life. This could be done through the final disposition of his fortune. His last will and testament would be the expression of his life's ideals. . . . The result was the most valued of prizes given to those who have done most for the cause of world peace.

from *Creative Brooding,*
edited by Robert A. Raines, p. 121.

The Little-Ease and the Spitting Cell
Albert Camus, author

I had to submit and admit my guilt. I had to live in the little-ease. To be sure, you are not familiar with that dungeon cell that was called the little-ease in the Middle Ages. In general, one was forgotten there for life. That cell was distinguished from others by ingenious dimensions. It was not high enough to stand up in nor yet wide enough to lie down in. One had to take on an awkward manner and live on the diagonal; sleep was a collapse, and waking a squatting. Mon cher, there was genius—and I am weighing my words—in that so simple invention. Every day through the unchanging restriction that stiffened his body, the condemned man learned that he was guilty and that innocence consists in stretching joyously. Can you imagine in that cell a frequenter of summits and upper decks? What? One could live in those cells and still be innocent? Improbable! Highly improbable! Or else my reasoning would collapse. That innocence should be reduced to living hunchbacked—I refuse to entertain for a second such a hypothesis. Moreover, we cannot assert the innocence of anyone, whereas we can state with certainty the guilt of all. . . .

Believe me, religions are on the wrong track the moment they moralize and fulminate commandments. God is not needed to create guilt or to punish. Our fellow men suffice aided by ourselves. You were speaking of the Last Judgment. . . . I shall wait for it resolutely, for I have known what is worse, the judgment of men. For them, no extenuating circumstances; even the good intention is ascribed to crime. Have you at least heard of the spitting cell, which a nation recently thought up to prove itself the greatest on earth? A walled-up box in which the prisoner can stand without moving. The solid door that locks him in his cement shell stops at chin level. Hence only his face is visible, and every passing jailer spits copiously on it. The prisoner, wedged into his cell, cannot wipe his face, though he is allowed, it is true, to close his eyes. Well, that, mon cher, is a human invention. They didn't need God for that little masterpiece.

What of it? Well, God's sole usefulness would be to guarantee innocence, and I am inclined to see religion rather as a huge laundering venture—as it was once but briefly, for exactly three years and it wasn't called religion. Since then, soap has been lacking, our faces are dirty, and we wipe one another's noses. All dunced, all punished, let's all spit on one another and—hurry! to the little-ease! Each tries to spit first, that's all. I'll tell you a big secret, mon cher. Don't wait for the Last Judgment. It takes place every day.

from *Creative Brooding,*
edited by Robert A. Raines, p. 51.

The Silent Father
Chaim Potok, author

"When I was very young, my father, may he rest in peace, began to wake me in the middle of the night, just so I would cry. I was a child, but he would wake me and tell me stories about the destruction of Jerusalem and the sufferings of the people of Israel, and I would cry. For years he did this. Once he took me to visit a hospital—ah, what an experience that was—and often he took me to visit the poor, the beggars, to listen to them talk. My father himself never talked to me, except when we studied together. He taught me with silence. He taught me to look into myself, to find my own strength, to walk around inside myself in company with my soul. When his people would ask him why he was so silent with his son, he would say to them that he did not like to talk, words are cruel, words play tricks, they distort what is in the heart, they conceal the heart, the heart speaks through silence. One learns of the pain of others by suffering one's own pain, he would say, by turning inside oneself, by finding one's own soul. And it is important to know of pain, he said. It destroys our self-pride, our arrogance, our indifference toward others. It makes us aware of how frail and tiny we are and of how much we must depend upon the Master of the Universe. Only slowly, very slowly, did I begin to understand what he was saying. For years his silence bewildered and frightened me, though I always trusted him, I never hated him. And when I was old enough to understand, he told me that of all people a *tzaddik* especially must know of pain. A *tzaddik* must know how to suffer for his people, he said. He must take their pain from them and carry it on his own shoulder. He must cry, in his heart he must always cry. Even when he dances and sings, he must cry for the sufferings of his people."

from *Soundings*,
edited by Robert A. Raines, p. 80.

Chapter 3

THE
LONELINESS

One of the hallmarks of the twentieth century has been the quest for a "religionless age," a society without God, an explanation of the meaning of life without faith. And what does such a world look like, smell like, taste like? As we come to the end of this century we now know. The singular word describing the conse- quence is . . . *empty*.

Christian people often forget what it is to swim in such an existence without lifeline or reprieve. The better we understand the emptiness, the more adept we are at articulating the answer.

One evening I looked out of the church office and saw a forlorn figure shuffling across the parking lot. Pastors, ministers, and priests become accustomed to panhandlers slithering in looking for an easy touch. Even when we know they are conning us, we clergy still struggle to find the right words.

But this man looked different.

The tattered figure was thin, the face gaunt. His feet barely cleared the pavement as he tottered forward. His eyes were empty and his mouth slightly open. He kept grimacing and shaking.

I listened more carefully than usual as the tall, skinny man tried to tell me what he wanted. He said his name was Jack and they were going to evict him. Jack was fifty and had no idea where to go or what to do. He wasn't desperate as much as hopeless. I quickly concluded he was clinically depressed and on the verge of suicide.

Jack's vacant stare became a mirror, and I took a second look at myself. There, but for the grace of God, went. . . .

Often we don't know what is right until everything has gone wrong. In the emptiness we remember what fullness meant.

A year earlier Jack's wife had died. With no children and the rest of his family gone, Mary was all he had in the whole world. When she died, his will to work, to play, to do anything . . . evaporated. Thirty days later the company fired him and Jack hadn't worked since. The center of his existence had crumbled. His soul died.

Different individuals experience loss in different ways. Listening to their discoveries brings us to our own awareness of what might be missing in our own lives.

Let's take another look at what the loss of soul is like. Listen to hollow voices, lonely sounds, and let the emptiness remind you of what was there.

Listen to voices that whistle down lonely streets like the winter wind on a cold forlorn night. The sounds of silence, the moans of failure, and the signs of loneliness, these statements are the conclusions of people who have lost the center of life.

———

Hollywood's a place where they'll pay you a thousand dollars for a kiss and fifty cents for your soul.

Marilyn Monroe

Truly one learns only by sorrow; it is a terrible education the soul gets, and it requires a terrible grief that shakes the very foundation of one's being to bring the soul into its own.

British Major Lanoe Hawker VC

Soul loss can be observed today as a psychological phenomenon in the everyday lives of the human beings around us. Loss of soul appears in the form of a sudden onset of apathy and listlessness; the joy has gone out of life, initiative is crippled, one feels empty, everything seems pointless.

Marie-Louise von Franz

I said, "But I beg you to give me some spiritual teaching. How can I save my soul?"

Anonymous

I know that there is no bandage that human beings can apply, no medicine for this open boundary, for my wounded soul.

Sue Nathanson-Elkin

A hundred, a thousand times a day, perhaps, "the soul is aborted."

Jacob Needleman

———

The Forlorn

Disconnectedness, isolation, and meaninglessness produces relentless loneliness. Loss of relationship with God, others, and ourselves leads to exile in the land of emotional drought—void of purpose, hope, caring, and love. These are the sounds of emptiness.

———

Loneliness is the anxiety that you do not matter at all.

Joyce Huggett

Loneliness is an unhappy compound of having lost one's point of reference, of suffering the fate of individual and collective discontinuity and of living through or dying from a crisis of identity to the point of alienation of one's self.

Dr. Ludwig Binswanger

We are all serving a life sentence in the dungeon of life.

Cyril Connolly

No one recovers from the disease of being born, a deadly wound if there ever was one.

Emile Cioran

Life is a dead-end street.

H. L. Mencken

Disillusionment

Somewhere between the innocence of childhood and the despair of old age, disillusionment settles over many like an emotional Alzheimer's disease. Joy gives way to cynicism and despondency reigns.

_____

Life is a wonderful thing to talk about, or to read about in history books—but it is terrible when one has to live it.

Jean Anouilh

Life is a disease; and the only difference between one man and another is the stage of the disease at which he lives.

George Bernard Shaw

Life is a zoo in a jungle.

Peter De Vries

Pity is for the living; envy is for the dead.

Mark Twain

I am leaving because I am bored.

George Sanders, in suicide note

To me death is not a fearful thing. It's living that's cursed.

Jim Jones, Jonestown, Guyana, 18 November 1978

I just have this feeling that our generation is dying away. There's Kurt [Cobain] and River Phoenix. The aimless quality of my age. The job situation. I think a lot of people think they're not understood, that their parents don't understand them, that society has no place for them because of their age.

Johanna Pirko, age 18

_____

In a real dark night of the soul it is always three o'clock in the morning.

F. Scott Fitzgerald

If the soul be lost, the man is lost.

John Flavel

The whole world cannot make up to a man for the loss of his soul.

J. C. Ryle

To live is the rarest thing in the world. Most people exist, that is all.

Oscar Wilde

We are always getting ready to live, but never living.

Ralph Waldo Emerson

The peculiar malaise of our day is air-conditioned un-happiness, the staleness and stuffiness of machine-made routine.

Rabbi Eugene Borowitz

There is nothing more tragic than to find an individual bogged down in the length of life, devoid of breadth.

Martin Luther King, Jr.

It is my conviction that a very large part of mankind's ills and of the world's misery is due to the rampant practice of trying to feed the soul with the body's food.

Frank Farrell

I live day to day, and life is a constant struggle that we win and lose on a daily basis.

Cher

Papillon, the French prisoner who was condemned to life imprisonment on Devil's Island, suffered from a recurring nightmare. Each night he would dream that he stood in judgment before a merciless tribunal. "You are charged," the words echoed, "with a wasted life. How do you plead?" In his dream he knelt in abject guilt and replied, "Guilty, I plead guilty."

Unknown

The Quest

Two doors open before meaninglessness and despair. One is marked "Nowhere" and the other "Promise." The first leads to oblivion, the other to recovery. The lonely must have the courage to persevere.

Desperately Searching for Spirituality
Timothy Jones, writer

A few years ago, Jack Simms of Baby Boomer Consulting in California predicted a "quest for spiritual meaning" by '90s boomers. That quest is a reality, even if it is taking on forms that the traditional church is not quite comfortable with.

Where does the church fit into this movement? Leonard Sweet, president of United Theological Seminary, defines the church's challenge as helping people "believe the right thing." The hunger for things spiritual is real, but the key, according to historian Martin Marty, is to turn that hunger from Twinkies to broccoli, from junk food to a transforming encounter with the God of the Bible.

from "Penchant for the Paranormal," pp. 1–2.

A Nation in Search of Spiritual Moorings
George Gallup, market researcher

In 1978, Alexander Solzhenitsyn warned America: "We have placed too much hope in politics and social reforms, only to find out that we were being deprived of our most precious possession: our spiritual life."

Today a look at surveys and trends reveals a new intensity in the search for spiritual meaning. Perhaps Americans have "hit bottom" and concluded, in their helplessness, that they need a higher power.

from "A Nation in Recovery," pp. 1–2.

We have become a generation of people who worship our work, who work at our play, and who play at our worship.

Charles Swindoll

The real value of an object is that which one who knows its worth will give for it. He who made the soul knew its worth, and gave his life for it.

Arthur Jackson

Your own soul is your first and greatest care.

Robert Murray M'Cheyne

None but God can satisfy the longings of the immortal soul; as the heart was made for him, he only can fill it.

Richard C. Trench

Chapter 4

SOUL-EATERS: SPIRITUAL CANNIBALISM

What does it look like when spiritual Draculas invade our town and lurk about on dark street corners? Not like the images of the old Bela Lugosi flicks of the 1930s. Instead, the pictures come pouring into our living rooms every night. Some estimates say children will see more than twenty-six thousand murders and acts of violence on television before they graduate from high school. We are surrounded by a culture of death. The result is a growing trivialization of suffering and human pain, along with an increasing acceptance of brutal violence as normal. Is such a shift anything other than a massive death of soul?

The time is long overdue to face the toll we pay for the spiritual cannibalism.

We have gained freedom without responsibility, prosperity without values, and affluence without spirituality. Our voyage through the twentieth century has taken us to ports of no return. Never has it become clearer that it is possible to gain the world and lose our souls!

Here's what the entertainment industry has to offer us.

"Are Music and Movies Killing America's Soul?"
Richard Lacayo, writer

At the Sherman Oaks multiplex, it's the same mixed bag. On the wide screens there's a face-off between the two top-grossing films of the week. *Casper* (the Friendly Ghost) offers his doe-eyed version of mortality against the merry bloodbath that is *Die Hard with a Vengeance*. But over at Taco Bell, 15-year-old Christopher Zahedi will tell you he prefers the rougher stuff. "I liked the part in *Pulp Fiction* where the guy points a gun and says a prayer from the Bible and then kills everybody," he offers. "You hear the gun go brrr. It's cool." . . .

By the early decades of the present century, there had emerged in the U.S. an entertainment industry that would eventually prove to be all-pervasive and ever more given to decking out our base impulses with sweaty and imaginative detail. It awaited only the youth culture that began stirring and shaking in the 1950s to take full advantage of the possibilities in rock, films and TV. The result was a pop culture more pointed and grown up, but also more shameless and adolescent; sometimes both at the same time. The great skirmishes against the blue-nosed guardians of culture—the Hays Office that policed movies in the '30s or the network censors who tormented the Smothers Brothers in the late '60s—became the stuff of baby boomer folklore. . . .

The complications set in during the '90s, when the

boomers who were once pop culture's most dedicated consumers became the decision makers at media companies—but also the parents of the next generation. Pulled one way by their lifelong instinct for whatever is sensational, unsanitized or unofficial, they find themselves dragged in the other direction by their emerging second thoughts as citizens and parents. . . .

In the aftermath of the Oklahoma City bombing, the conservatives are also struck with their own problem of violence in the media—and it's not just Schwarzenegger's body counts. "Jackbooted thugs," the description of federal law-enforcement agents in a fund-raising letter from the National Rifle Association, is a kind of cop-killer lyric in itself. So is "aim at the head"—radio talk-show host G. Gordon Liddy's suggestion for getting federal law-enforcement agents at your door."

Time, 12 June 1995, pp. 24–30.

Which is more threatening to America—the violence, obscenity, sexism and racism of movies and records, or the stark reality these movies and music reflect?

John Edgar Wideman, author and professor[1]

Yes, the entertainment industry is an empty, soulless empire. I can't bring myself to defend many of the films now made; I can't even defend those [Senator Robert] Dole approves of. Hollywood must examine itself. Its greed is sickening. It must judge the social impact, not just the popularity impact, of what it does. So must politicians who seek to exploit cultural values.

Paul Schrader, screenwriter and director[2]

I too dislike many pop-culture products, although probably not the ones that bother Senator Dole. But, the fact is, no system of regulation or voluntary restraint is going to have much effect on mass entertainment. And I'd like to hear how Dole squares his antiviolence stand with his ardent support for the N.R.A. and the overturning of the assault-weapons ban. Guns don't kill people; rap music kills people? Oliver Stone movies kill people? Please.

Katha Pollitt, poet, writer, and social critic[3]

Sadly, the U.S. has become the land of easy sex and uneasy souls.

Betsy Ross, New York City citizen,
from *Time-Forum*, 12 June 1995, pp. 32–35.

"America, What's Gone Wrong?"
William J. Bennett, author

The world still regards the United States as the leader in economic and military power, but no longer as the moral leader we once were.

Many foreigners come here believing they are visiting a degraded society, but violence and urban terror are only part of the picture. The ultimate insult from one immigrant student to another is, "You're becoming American." Foreign students are often more diligent and motivated than their American counterparts.

Though some of the criticisms of America that swept university campuses in the 1960s and 1970s were unjustified, we cannot deny some clear facts. While we live very well materially, we do not, as John Updike said, live *nobly*. In the past 30 years, our population has increased 41%, and government spending on social programs has risen from $142.7 billion to $787 billion, but we've seen a 560% increase in violent crime and a 400% rise in illegitimate births.

In the industrialized world, America ranks near the top in abortions, divorces, unwed births, and murder, but near the bottom in elementary and secondary school achievement scores. Other factors, not so easily seen or measured, also indicate decline. Morally, a coarseness, cynicism, and vulgarity now characterize our society. Yet our biggest problem is that we're not angry enough about these issues. We have become too accustomed to the cultural rot around us.

Many wish to blame liberal politicians, materialism, or consumerism for our decline. The real source, however, is an indifference, even an aversion, to spiritual matters. The effort to remove God from public life continues, and even privately, people are turning away from God. Historically, when millions of people stop believing in God, enormous public consequences follow.

Americans have put too much hope in politics as the solution to our problems. Politics can never cure moral and spiritual ills. In public policy, we say one thing and do another: e.g., we say we want law and order, yet allow violent criminals to return to the streets.

Until 25 years ago, the universally recognized goal of education was the moral and intellectual training of the young. We must return to that belief. We must return religion to its rightful place, both in individual lives and in society. We must refuse to accept the end of moral man; we must carry on the fight, pushing back against the evil forces that push hard against us, so we can save our children from the decadence of our time.

from *Current Thoughts and Trends,* July 1994, p. 24.

A Nation's Spiritual Decay
William J. Bennett, author

The Long Island Rail Road massacre in early December [1993] temporarily shook Americans. But the fact that it took a shower of bullets and a blood-splattered suburban railway car to get our attention speaks volumes about our complacency toward the crime and violence tearing our society apart.

Unfortunately, there are plenty of examples. A New York jury recently awarded a criminal $4.3 million. As he was fleeing the scene after a violent robbery attack that almost killed a 72-year-old man, a transit cop shot him in the back, paralyzing him. The thug won millions for his "pain and suffering"; the elderly man won a trip to the hospital. The public reaction was virtual silence.

During last year's Los Angeles riots, a news camera filmed Damian Williams and Henry Watson pulling an innocent man out of his truck, crushing his skull with a brick, and doing a victory dance over his fallen body. The lawyers of the young men obtained acquittals on most counts by building a legal defense on the proposition that individuals cannot be held accountable for getting caught up in mob violence. Much of the public wasn't irate, it was relieved.

These outward manifestations—and our complacency about them—are signs of a deeper decay. There is a coarseness, a callousness, a cynicism, a banality and a vulgarity to our time. There are too many signs of a civilization gone rotten. The worst of it has to do with our children: We live in a culture that at times almost seems dedicated to the corruption of the young, to ensuring the loss of their innocence before their time.

Pop culture plays a key role in this devaluing of America. An indicted murder suspect, Snoop Doggy Dog, recently saw his rap album "Doggystyle" debut at No. 1. On the daytime television talk shows, indecent exposure is celebrated as a virtue. In recent weeks these shows have dealt with: cross-dressing couples; a three-way love affair; a man whose chief aim in life is to sleep with women and fool them into thinking he is using a condom; women who can't say no to cheating; prostitutes who love their jobs; and an interview with a young girl caught in the middle of a bitter custody battle.

The real crisis of our time is spiritual. The ancients called it *acedia*—spiritual sloth or deadening, an undue concern for external affairs and worldly things and an absence of zeal for divine things. It eventually leads to a hatred of the good altogether.

When millions of people stop believing in God, or when their belief is so attenuated as to be belief in name only, enormous public consequences follow. We can achieve full employment and dynamic economic growth— we can build cities of gold and alabaster—but if our children have not learned to walk in goodness, justice and mercy, then the American experiment, no matter how gilded, will have failed.

Only when we turn our affections and desires toward the right things—toward enduring, noble, spiritual things—will our problems get better. . . .

Sadly, in America today the only respectable form of bigotry remaining is bigotry against religious people. If the ancients had a respect for the role religion plays in life, the moderns of our time hate religion because it forces them to confront matters they would prefer to ignore.

But we ignore them at our peril. It now requires a madman's sick episode of violence to touch us at our core. It is to that core we must attend.

from The Sower, Spring 1994, p. 10.

A Jewish Conservative Looks at Pagan America
Don Feder, author

When a rap song that calls for the murder of cops climbs to the top of the charts; when taxpayers are told that their objections to subsidizing a photograph of one man urinating into the mouth of another constitute censorship (when critics consecrate the same as the highest expression of the aesthetic); when a state's voters come within a hair's breadth of legalizing medical murder in the name of relieving suffering; when a presidential candidate informs voters that whether or not he violated his marriage vows is none of their business, we may as well declare intellectual bankruptcy and have the nation placed in moral receivership.

from Discipleship Journal, September/October 1993, p. 16.

America has a serious problem when $25 can buy a gun and end a life.

Adam Bitner, Barrington, Ill. citizen,
from "Letters to the Editor," Time, 23 August 1993.

Bang! You're Dead, America!
Youthworker Update, November 1994

In 1991 alone, bullets deprived Americans of 1.1 million years of potential life. Fatalities from gunshot wounds are the fourth leading cause of premature death. Only injuries, cancer, and heart disease take more lives. (The Centers for Disease Control and Prevention arrived at the 1.1 million figure by subtracting the age of gunshot victims from a life expectancy of 65 years.)

The fact that [my] column has been a success underscores, for me at least, the central tragedy of our society, the disconnectedness, the insecurity, the fear that bedevils, cripples, and paralyzes so many of us. I have learned that financial success, academic achievement, and social or political status open no doors to peace of mind or inner security. We are all wanderers, like sheep, on this planet. . . .

Suicide is the second most frequent cause of death among teenagers in this country. (The first is accidents.) Every 90 minutes a teenager in America will kill himself. I am firmly against censorship, but where is the moral outrage against all the filth? It's almost impossible to find a family movie these days. What has happened to plain, everyday decency?

As John Underwood wrote so eloquently in the *Boston Globe* a while back, "Civilizations do not give out, they give *in*. In a society where anything goes, eventually, everything will."

from *Current Thoughts and Trends,* January 1995, p. 33.

"We Must Learn Why Are We Producing Such Violent People"
William Raspberry, newspaper columnist

I don't want to convict the two eighteen-year-olds charged in the death of Michael Jordan's father. It'll be a while before we know whether the prosecutors can make the case they've been laying out to reporters.

But we already know enough about the two suspects, Larry Demery and Daniel Green, to wonder where such kids come from—and how we can stop producing more of them. And—please—let's not chalk it up to poverty.

The North Carolina authorities say the two boys (both indisputably poor) came upon James Jordan's $46,000 Lexus, with the 56-year-old owner asleep in the front seat, killed him, and drove away in his car. Later, according to the police, they disposed of the body and later abandoned the car. They were identified after police were able to trace the calls the two allegedly made on the car phone.

These are not first offenders. Mr. Demery's record includes a string of 14 burglaries, forgeries and larcenies, most of which never even came to trial. He was to have been tried this month for what, until the Jordan murder, had been his most serious charge: an October 1992 robbery in which he allegedly bashed a 61-year-old convenience store clerk over the head with a cinder block. Police say he was carrying a pistol at the time.

Mr. Green's career highlight came three years ago, when he took an ax to the head of a classmate—reportedly in a fight over a girl. The boy he assaulted spent a year in a hospital, several months of it in a coma. He still suffers seizures.

Mr. Green was sentenced to six years for assault with a deadly weapon with intent to kill. He was paroled two months ago after serving two years.

Where do these kids come from? The judicial system, bad schools, inadequate parenting and, of course, poverty will get their share of the blame. But there is something more.

There is a generational, ethical and cultural divide that keeps some of us from understanding the rest of us. Some of us (still the majority?) cannot imagine shooting anyone else except to protect our own life or that of a loved one—not for a million dollars, let alone for the short-term thrill of driving a Lexus. We cannot imagine smashing a cinder block over some woman's head in order to make off with seven dollars and a pocketful of cheap jewelry. We cannot imagine gunning down rivals, except in self-defense, and certainly we cannot imagine killing strangers because they have something we want.

And yet there are growing numbers of youngsters who will kill for leather jackets or a pair of sneakers. How do they get that way?

Maybe it's time to start asking how we on the civil side of the divide got to be the way we are. The two main reasons, I suspect, are that we are brought up that way and that it has worked for us.

We were taught sharing and civility so early and so thoroughly that our natural urges to selfishness and rage are kept in check. We were taught to view ourselves not merely as winners or chumps but as moral creatures, for whom decent behavior is an important (though often inconvenient) value.

And it has worked. Probably the key reason we respect the person and property of others is the expectation—that our person and property will be respected.

What happens when these values aren't taught early, and when people grow up never feeling respected?

I am not saying—because I don't know—that the parents of the boys charged in the Jordan killing failed to give them the necessary moral foundation, or that they didn't learn respect because they weren't respected.

I'm not even arguing for leniency; I want kids like this off the street as much as anyone else.

But I also know that we can't cure the problem of escalating violence merely by trying to keep the already-violent off the street. We have neither the hope of reforming them nor the prison space to incarcerate them forever. Even the death penalty advocates don't want to kill all violent offenders. Sooner or later, most of the already-violent will be back on the street, at least as dangerous as before.

If we are to save ourselves, we will have to learn to turn off the spigot that keeps spewing new violence-prone youngsters. We've got to teach them early as we were taught the values that make civilized society possible, and we've got to show them that our values work.

Locking up those whose violence mocks our attitudes and beliefs may be necessary but it's not enough. We've got to re-create ourselves.

from *The Dallas Morning News,* 23 August 1993, p. 13A.

Most people sell their souls, and live with a good conscience on the proceeds.

Logan Pearsall Smith

Sin is whatever obscures the soul.

André Gide

If you are losing your leisure, look out; you may be losing your soul.

Logan Pearsall Smith

The tragedy of life is what dies inside a man while he lives.

Albert Einstein

The danger is not lest the soul should doubt whether there is any bread, but lest, by a lie, it should persuade itself that it is not hungry.

Simone Weil

What are some conclusions we might draw in the face of such overwhelming evidence that we live in an age of spiritual cannibalism?

Listen to a parable.

The Soul-Eater
A West African Folktale

Once there was an old man who had four sons. One was a soldier, one a hunter, one a farmer, and the youngest one lived in a nearby town and had no work. The father lived in a large forest with the hunter and the farmer.

One day, the hunter set out with his gun to provide meat for the family. He trapped an animal that looked like a giant rat and carried it back to the compound. As soon as the father saw the animal he told his son that they must not eat it because it was not an ordinary animal but one which had the power to eat a man's soul.

The boy laughed at his father, saying, "Old men are as superstitious as old women. Meat is meat, Pa, and I intend to eat this animal."

The father said nothing more but went out to tap some palmwine. While he was out, the hunter skinned his prey and put it on the fire to cook.

When Papa returned his son told him, "Hey Pa, I threw out that other meat and I am now cooking a goat. Come and eat."

Still Papa refused, and he advised his other son not to eat the meat either. The meat smelt very good, but only the hunter ate it, and he ate and ate until he had eaten it all.

Next morning the father called his farmer son and told him that they must go out hunting. The farmer went to waken his brother but the brother did not move. The farmer pulled and shook his brother but he did not move. He looked as if he were only sleeping but he was not breathing. The farmer felt very sad and went outside to dig a grave.

While he was digging his father came out and said, "Why are you digging a grave? Your brother is not dead. Leave him where he is."

The farmer was annoyed with his father. "Pa," he insisted, "my brother is dead. I cannot just leave his body in the house to corrupt. I must bury him. He's dead, Pa."

Papa just looked at his son. "You young men," he said, "you think you know everything. Your brother wouldn't listen to me yesterday and today you won't listen."

The brother stopped digging and followed his father into the forest. They saw a tiger but Papa said, "We are not hunting tigers."

They saw a leopard but Papa said, "We are not hunting leopards."

All day they searched and each time they saw an animal Papa refused to hunt it, until they saw one that looked like a giant rat. "This is the animal we must hunt," said the father.

He and his son struggled with the animal, which cried like a child each time they hit it. At last the father hit it a mighty blow on the skull and it died. The farmer bent to pick it up but his father insisted, "Don't touch it. Leave it where it is."

The son and his father went home. They found the hunter lying in blood with his skull cracked open. "Now you can bury him," said the father.

And the farmer buried his brother and wondered at the wisdom of old men.

from *Tortoise the Trickster and Other Folktales from Cameroon*, edited by Loretto Todd, pp. 65–66.

Chapter 5

THE
CONTEMPORARY
HUNGER

Above the empty noise of the clogged streets of modern megalopolis, voices can still be heard crying out for what has been lost. The poets, writers, artists, and soul people in this impersonal age know there is more to life than what they can see around them. Such searchers will not settle for the emptiness of the multitudes struggling off to the grave without much assurance they were ever really alive.

An anthology of this quest helps give us a feel of where many people are looking today. These assembled works better enable us to get in touch with our own center. Musing through such writings also better enables us to ask about where the inner place of our soul might be.

From the past several centuries, these chasers after God and personhood tell us about the haunts visited in their desperate search for meaning. Some ask the question in religious language and others are thoroughly secular. Either way, they are scouting the same terrain.

Let's listen for the cries in the night, the moans of pain over lost love and destroyed destiny as well as the aaahs and oohs when discovery has been rich. These humans have not yet given up on humanity.

Looking for More

Nothing Lost
**Mircea Eliade, Romanian-American
religious historian, 1907–1987**

What impressed me the most in my conversations with Teilhard de Chardin was his response to the question that I had asked him: What did the immortality of the soul mean for him? Difficult to summarize. Briefly: according to T. de Ch., everything that can be transmitted and communicated (love, culture, politics, etc.) "does not pass into the beyond" but disappears with the death of the individual. But there remains an irreducible, incommunicable foundation, or, more precisely, what is impossible to express or communicate—and it is this mysterious, incalculable foundation that "passes into the beyond" and survives the disappearance of the body. An interesting theory because it appears to imply that if we succeeded someday in communicating and transmitting *absolutely all* human experiences, immortality would become useless and would then cease. What interested Father Teilhard was the principle of the conservation of human experiences. Nothing must be lost. All experience must be expressed (by language by culture), and it is thus recorded and kept in the noosphere.

from *No Souvenirs,* pp. 99–100.

Streams in the Soul
Rudolf Steiner, German anthroposophist, 1861–1925

Anyone who looks deeply into the life of the soul will see that these two streams, one from the past and one from the future, are continually meeting there. The fact that we are influenced by the past is obvious: Who could deny that our energy or idleness of yesterday has some effect on us today? But we ought not to deny the reality of the future, either, for we can observe in the soul the intrusion of future events, although they have not yet happened. After all, there is such a thing as fear of something likely to happen tomorrow, or anxiety about it. Is that not a sort of feeling or perception concerned with the future? Whenever the soul experiences fear or anxiety, it shows by the reality of its feelings that it is reckoning not only with the past but in a very lively manner with something hastening towards it from the future. These, of course, are single examples, but they will find numerous others to contradict the abstract logic which says that since the future does not yet exist, it can have no present influence.

Thus there are these two streams, one from the past and one from the future, which come together in the soul—will anyone who observes himself deny that?—and produce a kind of whirlpool, comparable to the confluence of two rivers. Closer observation shows that the impressions left on us by past experiences, and in which we have dealt with them, have made the soul what it is. We bear within ourselves the legacy of our doing, feeling, and thinking in the past. If we look back over these past experiences, especially those in which we played an active part, we shall very often be impelled to an assessment of ourselves. . . .

We need only to remember the feelings of fear and anxiety that gnaw at our soul-life in face of the unknown future. Is there anything that can give the soul a sense of security in this situation? Yes, there is. It is what we may call a feeling of humbleness towards anything that may come towards the soul out of the darkness of the future. But this feeling will be effective only if it has the character of prayer. Let us avoid misunderstanding. We are not extolling something that might be called humbleness in one sense or another; we are describing a definite form of it—humbleness to whatever the future may bring. Anyone who looks anxiously and fearfully toward the future hinders his development, hampers the free unfolding to his soul-forces. Nothing, indeed, obstructs this development more than fear and anxiety in face of the unknown future. But the results of submitting to the future can be judged only by experience. What does this humbleness mean?

Ideally, it would mean saying to oneself: Whatever the next hour or day may bring. I cannot change it by fear or anxiety, for it is not yet known. I will therefore wait for it with complete inward restfulness, perfect tranquility of mind. Anyone who can meet the future in this calm, relaxed way, without impairing his active strength and energy, will be able to develop the powers of his soul freely and intensively.

from *Metamorphoses of the Soul*, Vol. 2, pp. 43–45.

A Child's Question

Robert Coles, psychiatrist and author

"When I wake up early, and our dog really wants to go out, and he leaps on my bed, and I know he won't let me go back to sleep, I just know it—he'll lick my face, and he'll whine, and he'll lean against me hard, real hard—and when I give up and take him out, and I just stand there, and it's still dark, and you can hear your dog sniffing, it's that quiet: It's then I know there's someone up there, maybe God, maybe lots of people, too, the souls of all the dead folks. It's too big for you to figure out. My dad tells me that when I ask him about God and where heaven is and if there's a soul. He says there is *definitely* a soul, but it's not 'physical,' so I shouldn't keep asking him, 'Where is it?'

"He's right; you can ask too many questions! That's me—always trying to find out answers to everything! I wish you *could* find them. In the last year or so, I've sort of slowed down asking! I just look up there and say, 'Maybe!' I was walking our dog in the park, there—*souls* out there—and they must want to talk with someone. I guess they talk with each other. But how? Where are they? Dad says he thinks when you die, your soul dies with you. But then, it's not a soul, it's your mind he's talking about, isn't it? It's probably best just to forget everything except what you have to do today: and the same thing with to-morrow. The only thing is, when you go to Hebrew school and *schul* [synagogue], they tell you God is with us, the Jews, and your soul is His gift to you, that's what the rabbi told us kids when he visited our classroom, and I was going to ask him where in your body God puts the soul He gives you, but I decided that I'd be getting myself into real trouble, because the Hebrew school teacher says I ask too many questions, and I should learn Hebrew and read from Torah and stop trying to be a 'philosopher king.' Well, what's that? Yes, I asked. The teacher didn't think it was funny, my question [as he and I did]. He said, 'No more questions!' If I'd raised my hand like that, when the rabbi came to visit our class, I think the teacher would have taken that [blackboard] point of his and charged me with it, like in the Middle Ages, when the knights went after each other with swords or spears."

from *The Spiritual Life of Children*.

Tenderness, Soul, and Saint Teresa
Raymond Carver, American author, 1939–1988

There is a line of prose from the writings of Saint Teresa which seemed more and more appropriate as I thought toward this occasion, so I want to offer a meditation on that sentence. It was used as an epigraph to a recent collection of poems by Tess Gallagher, take the line from the context of her epigraph.

Saint Teresa, that extraordinary woman who lived 373 years ago, said: "Words lead to deeds. . . . They prepare the soul, make it ready, and move it to tenderness."

There is clarity and beauty in that thought expressed in just this way. I'll say it again, because there is also something a little foreign in this sentiment coming to our attention at this remove, in a time certainly less openly supportive of the important connection between what we say and what we do: "Words lead to deeds. . . . They prepare the soul, make it ready, and move it to tenderness."

There is something more than a little mysterious, not to say—forgive me—even mystical about these particular words and the way Saint Teresa used them, with full weight and belief. True enough, we realize they appear almost as echoes of some former, more considered time.

Especially the mention of the word "soul," a word we don't encounter much these days outside of church and perhaps in the "soul" section of the record store.

"Tenderness"—that's another word we don't hear much these days, and certainly not on such a public, joyful occasion as this. Think about it: When was the last time you used the word or heard it used? It's in a short supply as that other word, "soul."

There is a wonderfully described character named Moiseika in Chekhov's story "Ward No. 6" who, although he has been consigned to the madhouse wing of the hospital, has picked up the habit of a certain kind of tenderness. Chekhov writes: "Moiseika likes to make himself useful. He gives his companions water, and covers them up when they are asleep; he promises each of them to bring him back a kopeck, and to make him a new cap; he feeds with a spoon his neighbor on the left, who is paralysed."

Even though the word tenderness isn't used, we feel its presence in these details, even when Chekhov goes on to enter a disclaimer by way of this commentary on Moiseika's behavior: "He acts in this way, not from compassion nor from any considerations of a humane kind, but through imitation, unconsciously dominated by Gromon, his neighbor on the right hand."

In a provocative alchemy, Chekhov combines words and deeds to cause us to reconsider the origin and nature of tenderness. Where does it come from? As a deed, does it still move the heart, even when abstracted from humane motives?

Somehow, the image of the isolated man performing gentle acts without expectation or even self-knowledge stays before us as an odd beauty we have been brought to witness. It may even reflect back upon our own lives with a questioning gaze.

There is another scene from "Ward No. 6" in which two characters, a disaffected doctor and an imperious post-master, his elder, suddenly find themselves discussing the human soul.

"And you do not believe in the immortality of the soul?" the postmaster asks suddenly.

"No, honoured Mihail Averyanitch; I do not believe it, and have no grounds for believing it."

"I must own I doubt it, too," Mihail Averyanitch admits. "And yet I have a feeling as though I should never die. Oh, I think to myself: 'Old fogey, it is time you were dead!' But there is a little voice in my soul says: 'Don't believe it; you won't die.'"

The scene ends but the words linger as deeds. "A little voice in the soul" is born. Also the way we have perhaps dismissed certain concepts about life, about death, sud-denly gives over unexpectedly to belief of an admittedly fragile but insistent nature.

Long after what I've said has passed from your minds, whether it be weeks or months, and all that remains is the sensation of having attended a public occasion, marking the end of one significant period of your lives and the beginning of another, try then, as you work out your individual destinies, to remember that words, the right true words, can have the power of deeds.

Remember, too, that little-used word that has just about dropped out of public and private usage: tenderness. It can't hurt. And that other word: soul—call it spirit if you want, if it makes it any easier to claim the territory.

from *No Heroics, Please.*

Ancient Longings

The wind, one brilliant day, called
Antonio Machado, Spanish poet, 1875–1939

The wind, one brilliant day, called
to my soul with an aroma of jasmine.
"In return for this jasmine odor,
I'd like all the odor of your roses."
"I have no roses; I have no flowers left now
in my garden . . . All are dead."
"Then I'll take the waters of the fountains,
and the yellow leaves and the dried-up petals."
The wind left . . . I wept. I said to my soul,
"What have you done with the garden entrusted to
    you?"

from *Times Alone: Selected Poems of Antonio Machado.*

Facing the World with Soul
Robert Sardello, American psychotherapist

By soul wisdom I mean the development of a capacity for self-knowledge in conjunction with an objective sense of the inner qualities of the outer world. The capacity for this conjunction leads to a new image of consciousness that "sees through" events, both inner and outer, finding a circulation going on between them in which a constant re-creation of both the human being and the world takes place. This circulating force or power I shall call soul, and to make clear that what I am calling soul has little to do with individual life alone, by soul I shall always imply *the soul of the world* as a way of referring to the inseparable conjunction of individual and world: and further, this is always a conjunction in depth. . . .

When the ancient seers looked up on the world, what did they see? They saw magic. One can still see that today if one knows how to look. The seer might be walking in a forest and see among all the trees a birch—because the birch is such a conspicuous tree. It is unbelievably supple. With her beautiful white trunk she stands, yielding to the slightest movement of air, swaying amongst the more woody and unbending trees such as the oaks and beeches. No matter how old a big birch becomes, the suppleness is retained. And she does not allow herself to be overgrown. Drawing up enormous amounts of water through her roots, the birch effectively drains the ground. The seer sees these qualities and thus sees the gifts of the birch. She is wonderful medicine; since she is able to keep at bay all hardening tendencies, the birch can assist in keeping body tissues soft and supple. Because the birch drains as well she offers an effective diuretic. But we need not conclude from this example that the way to Sophia is the return to nature. It is not so much the birch that is important as it is the way of seeing the birch, seeking the magic in the birch, its soul qualities. Magic, then, is the soul of the world creating itself, according to its own laws . . .

Now, there is magic and there is the magic of the soul of the world. Christopher Marlowe's *Faust* presents the archetypal image of individual magic, the usurpation of the realm of the magic of the world by the need for control. Faust reveals an image of elitism, of one who sought special privileges for himself and the means to obtain them. Magic here becomes the way to power, to accomplishment without responsibility, the degradation of soul wisdom to individual omnipotence . . .

The magical tradition, when not corrupted, never concerns an interest in personal power, but rather the passage through three gateways leading to the capacity for perception of the world soul. The first gateway concerns remembering the ancestors, passing into living relation with the ancestors. The second gateway concerns passing into a living relation with archetypal beings, and the third gateway gives passage into the soul substance of the land. Rather than coming to personal power, through these activities humans become mediators between the ancestral and archetypal beings and the archetypal substance of the land.

from *Facing the World with Soul*, pp. 20–22.

The Legend of St. Elmo's Fire
Edward Corbiere, 1832
From the journal of a nineteenth-century sailor

During a stormy night one noticed on board fires that played at each end of our main yard. This bright and blue flame, like those that one lights on a punch that is served in cafes, aroused my curiosity for the first time.

"What on earth is that?" I asked a sailor in amazement.

"Saint Elmo's fire, sir."

"Ah, yes, it burns!"

"One had better say that is the sailor's friend. Do you see that kind of flame? Well, if the officer of the watch told me 'Climb up by yourself, pull down the small topsail' [which is in fact quite heavy for just one man], I would pull it down on the double because that fire would go

.with me up the rigging to help me, as it helps all sailors."

"But how can you take such a story seriously? It is quite simply, as I remember having read, a natural effect, an electrical discharge that, like a fluid of this kind, seeks points."

"How can I believe that story? An effect of *lubricity*, *electrical* discharge, as you please. But it is no less true that that fire, which resembles a glass of brandy that is alight, is the soul of a poor sailor who drowned in the sea in a storm. So you see, when the weather is about to get worse, the soul of the sailors who have taken one drink too many from the great pond, comes and warns their comrades that a dangerous storm is approaching."

"My word, just in case it is true I want to see if I can touch the soul of a dead man, and I shall go straight to the running board of the yardarm to catch up with your Saint Elmo's fire."

I climbed to the end of the yardarm, as I had said I would, to the great surprise of my companion, who saw a kind of profanation in the intention that I had of going needlessly to bother what he called the sailor's friend.

As my hand gradually got closer to the Saint Elmo's fire, the fluid moved up and down and away and did not come back until I had withdrawn it. This sort of little war between it and myself greatly amused the men of the watch, and they said to me again and again:

"Oh, that one is meaner than you or us."

A sailor from the Lower Brittany cried out to me: "Do you want me to make it disappear?"

"Yes," I replied.

And he made the sign of the cross. The fire did indeed vanish at that very moment . . .

from *The Slave Trader*, pp. 43–45.

The Black Experience

Soul Snatchers
Alice Walker, African American author

Sometime during the early seventies I was asked to write a letter to an imaginary young black woman, giving her some sense of my own experiences and telling her things she might need to know. I wrote a long letter, which I sent off to the person who asked for it. (I no longer recall who this was), but then discovered I wanted to say even more.

Dear Joanna:

Forgive me for writing again so soon. I realize you are busy reading the words of all your other sisters who also love you, but you have been constantly on my mind each day. I think of new things to share with you. Today I wanted to tell you about beauty.

In you, there is beauty like a rock.

So distilled, so unshatterable, so ageless, it will attract great numbers of people who will attempt, almost as an exercise of will (and of no more importance to them that an exercise), to break it. They will try ignoring you, flattering you, joining you, buying you, simply to afford themselves the opportunity of finding the one crack in your stone of beauty by which they may enter with their tools of destruction. Often you will be astonished that, while they pursue their single-minded effort to do this, they do not seem to see your sorrowing face (sorrowing because some of them will have come to you in the disguise of friends, even sisters) or note the quavering of your voice, or the tears of vulnerability in your eyes. To such people, your color, your sex, your*self* make you an object. But an object, strangely, perversely, with a soul. A soul.

It is your soul they want.

They will want to crack it out of the rock and wear it somewhere—not inside them, where it might do them good, but *about* them—like, for example, a feather through their hair, or a scalp dangling from their belt.

As frightening as this is, it has always been so.

Your mother and father, your grandparents, *their* parents, all have had your same beauty like a rock, and all have been pursued, often hunted down like animals, because of it. Perhaps some grew tired of resisting, and in weariness relinquished the stone that was their life. But most resisted to the end. The end, for them, being merely you. Your life. Which is not an end.

That resistance is your legacy.

Inner beauty, an irrepressible music, certainly courage to say No or Yes, dedication to one's own Gods, affection for one's own spirit(s), a simplicity of approach to life, will survive all of us through your will.

You are, perhaps, the last unconquered resident on this earth. And must live, in any case, as if it *must* be so.

from *Living by the Word Selected Writings*, pp. 75–78.

Soul Food
Sheila Ferguson, African American singer and author

Ah, soul food. Soul is just what the name implies. It is soulfully cooked food or richly flavored foods good for your ever-loving soul. But soul food is much more than a clever name penned by some unknown author. It is a legacy clearly steeped in tradition; a way of life that has been handed down from generation to generation, from one black family to another, by word of mouth and sleight of hand. It is rich in both history and variety of flavor.

To cook soul food you must use all of your senses. You cook by instinct but you also use smell, taste, touch, sight, and particularly, sound. You learn to hear by the crackling sound when it's time to turn over the fried chicken, to smell when a pan of biscuits is just about to finish baking, and to feel when a pastry's just right to the touch. You taste, rather than measure, the seasonings you treasure; and you use your eyes, not a clock, to judge when that cherry pie has bubbled sweet and nice. These skills are hard to teach quickly. They must be felt, loving, and come straight from the heart and soul.

Ah, but when you taste good soul food then it'll take hold of your soul and hang your unsuspecting innards out to dry. It's that shur'nuf everlovin' down-home stick-to-your-ribs kinda food that keeps you glued to your seat long after the meal is over and done with, enabling you to sit back, relax, and savor the gentle purrings of a well satisfied stomach, feeling that all's right with the world. Yes suh! As the good Baptist minister says every Sunday morning. Yes suh!

Let me give you a for instance. Say you fry up a batch of fresh chicken to a golden-brown crispness, but you keep the insides so moist, so tender, that all that good juice just bursts forth with the first crunchy bite. Then maybe you bake up some cornbread and buttermilk biscuits, ready to smother with freshly churned butter, and you cook up a big pot of collard greens and pot likka seasoned with ham hocks, onion, vinegar, red pepper flakes, and just enough hot sauce to set fire to your palate. Just a little fire though! Now you pile on a mound of slightly chilled home-made potato salad and fill a pitcher full of ice-cold lemonade ready to cool out that fire. And when you've eaten your way through all of that, you finish it off with a healthy hunk of pecan pie topped with a scoop of homemade vanilla ice cream. Now, tell me the truth—do you think you could move after a meal like that? Only for second helpings, of course!

But that's just the fun-loving, toe-tapping, belly-busting, knee-slapping, thirst-quenching, foot-stomping side of a cuisine that has its more serious side too. For the basic frame work of this style of cooking was carved out in the deep South by the black slaves, in part for their white masters and in part for their own survival in the slave quarters. As such, it is, like the blues of jazz, an inextricable part of the black Americans' struggle to survive and to express themselves. In this sense it is a *true* American cuisine, because it wasn't imported into America by immigrants like so many other ethnic offerings. It is the cuisine of the American, if you like. Because what can't be cured must be endured. As John Egerton so aptly puts it in *Southern Food,*

> In the most desolate and hopeless of circumstances, blacks caught in the grip of slavery often exhibited uncommon wisdom, beauty, strength, and creativity. The kitchen was one of the few places where their imagination and skill could have free rein and full expression, and there they often excelled. From the elegant breads and meats and sweets of plantation cookery to the inventions of Creole cuisine, from beaten biscuits to bouillabaisse, their legacy of culinary excellence is all the more impressive, considering the extremely adverse conditions under which it was compiled.

Rations were usually once a week, on Saturday nights, and then the righteous jubilation would commence in the slave quarters. The slaves pretty much insisted on having Sundays as their day to worship. Of course, no alcohol was allowed. Don't be ridiculous! It was alright for white folk, but bad for African and American Indian blood. However, that didn't matter. The slaves had their own way to lift up their souls. They would pray, they would sing, and they would eat!

from *Soul Food*, pp. 1–2.

Soul Music
Peter Guralnick, journalist

This is what I mean today when I am talking about soul music. Soul music is Southern by definition if not by actual geography. Like the blues, jazz, and rock 'n' roll, both its birth and inspiration stem from the South, so that while Solomon Burke, one of the very greatest of soul singers, is a native of Philadelphia, and Garnet Mimms, a little appreciated but nearly equally talented vocalist, made many of his recordings there, the clear inspiration for the styles of both is the Southern revivalism that fueled such diverse figures as Elvis Presley and Hank Williams on the one hand, Little Richard and Ray Charles on the other. I do believe there's a regional philosophy involved here, too, whether it's the agrarian spirit cited by Jerry Wexler ("There was always this attitude, 'Oh, man, we're gonna lose our soul if we do that. We're not gonna let machinery kill our natural Southern thing.'"), or simply the idea that Dan Penn, the renegade white hero of this book, has frequently expressed: "People down here don't let nobody tell them what to do." Unquestionably the racial turmoil of the South was a factor, and the rapid social upheaval which it foreshadowed; in fact, the whole tangled racial history of the region, the intimate terms on which it lived with its passions and contradictions, played a decisive role in the forging of a new culture, one which the North's polite lip service to liberalism could never have achieved. Ultimately soul music derives, I believe, from the Southern dream of freedom.

It is not, however (contrary to most received opinion), a music of uninhibited emotional release—though at times it comes close. What it offers, rather, is something akin to the "knowledgeable apprehension," in Alfred Hitchcock's famous definition of suspense, that precedes the actual climax, that everyone knows is coming—it's just nobody is quite sure when. Soul music is a music that keeps hinting at a conclusion, keeps straining at the boundaries—of melody and convention—that it has imposed upon itself. That is where it is to be differentiated from the let-it-all-hang-out rock 'n' roll of a cheerful charismatic like Little Richard, who for all the brilliance of his singing and the subtleties of which he is capable, basically hits the ground running and accelerates from there. It is which, with equal claim to inspiration from the church, rarely uncorks a full-blooded scream, generally establishes the tension without ever really letting go, and only occasionally will reveal a flash of raw emotion. This is not because Motown singers were not equally talented or equally capable of revealing their true feelings; it is simply that Motown was an industry aimed specifically at reaching the white market, and every aspect of that industry was controlled, from the grooming and diction of its stars to the subtlest interpolations on its records. Southern soul music, on the other hand, was a haven for free-lancers and individualists. It was a musical mode in which the band might be out of tune, the drummer out of time, the singer off-key, and yet the message could still come across—since underlying feeling was all. Feeling dictated the rhythm, feeling dictated the pace; that is why soul remains to this day so idiosyncratic a domain. One of the most common fallacies of a postapocalyptic age such as ours is that there is no room for anything *but* the dramatic gesture; modulation is something as unheard-of as self-restraint. Soul music, which might in one sense be considered a herald of the new age, knew differently in the 1960s, and among the most surprising aspects of going back and listening to the music today— among its most enduring qualities—are the quiet moments at the center, the moments of stillness where action stops and "knowledgeable" anticipation takes over. Think of the great screams you've heard from everyone from James Brown to Wilson Pickett; think of the fervor of Solomon Burke's or Jo Tex's preaching on subjects as far removed in substance and seriousness as "skinny legs and all" or the price that love can exact. In gospel music, the progenitor of the style, a singer is often described as "worrying" the audience, teasing it, working the crowd until it is on the verge of exploding, until strong men faint and women start speaking in tongues. This is commonly referred to as "house wrecking."

from *Sweet Soul Music*, pp. 6–8.

A Soul Aching for God

Tragically, the consummate English poet Francis Thompson (1859–1907) anticipated the late twentieth century's hunger for God in more than one way. In a time before the devastating power of opium and morphine were fully understood, Thompson became a drug addict. The sensitive mind and soul of the poet could not escape the ravages of the drug. But even more, Thompson came to understand no condition of debasement would escape the pursuit of the love of God. The following excerpt is the final plea of a desperate soul.

The Hound of Heaven
Francis Thompson

I fled Him, down the nights and down the days;
   I fled Him down the arches of the years;
I fled Him down the labyrinthine ways
   Of my own mind; and in the mist of tears
I hid from Him, and under running laughter.
      Up vistaed hopes I sped;
      And shot, precipitated,
   Adown titanic glooms of chasmed fears,
From those strong Feet that followed, followed after.
      But with unhurrying chase
      And unperturbed pace,
   Deliberate speed, majestic instancy,
      They beat—and a Voice beat
      More instant than the Feet—
"All things betray thee, who betrayest Me."

   I pleaded, out law-wise,
By many a hearted casement, curtained red,
   Trellised with intertwining charities;
(For, though I knew His love Who followed,
      Yet I was sore adread
Lest, having Him, I must have naught beside;)

But, if one little casement parted wide,
　　The gust of His approach would clash it to.
　　Fear wist not to evade, as Love wist to pursue.
Across the margent of the world I fled,
　　And troubled the gold gateways of the stars,
　　Smiting for shelter on their clanged bars;
　　　Fretted to dulcet jars
And silvern chatter the pale ports o' the moon.
I said to dawn, Be sudden; to eve, Be soon;
　　With thy young skyey blossoms heap me over
　　　From this tremendous Lover!
Float thy vague veil about me, lest He see!
　　I tempted all His servitors, but to find
My own betrayal in their constancy,
In faith to Him their fickleness to me,
　　Their traitorous trueness, and their loyal deceit.
To all swift things for swiftness did I sue;
　　Clung to the whistling mane of every wind.
　　　But whether they swept, smoothly fleet,
　　The long savannahs of the blue;
　　　Or whether, Thunder-driven,
　　They clanged His chariot 'thwart a heaven
Plashy with flying lightnings round the spurn o' their
　　　　feet:—
　　Fear wist not to evade as Love wist to pursue.
　　　Still with unhurrying chase
　　　And unperturbed pace,
　　Deliberate speed, majestic instancy,
　　　Came on the following Feet,
　　　And a Voice above their beat—
"Naught shelters thee, who wilt not shelter Me."

．　．　．　．　．　．　．　．　．　．　．　．

In vain my tears were wet on Heaven's grey cheek.
For ah! we know not what each other says,
 These things and I; in sound *I* speak—
Their sound is but their stir, they speak by silences.
Nature, poor stepdame, cannot slake my drouth;
 Let her, if she would owe me,
Drop yon blue bosom-veil of sky, and show me
 The breasts o' her tenderness:

Never did any milk of hers once bless
 My thirsting mouth.
 Nigh and nigh draws the chase
 With unperturbed pace,
Deliberate speed, majestic instancy;
 And past those noised Feet
A voice comes yet more fleet—
"Lo, naught contents thee, who content'st not Me."

. . . .

 Halts by me that footfall:
 Is my gloom, after all,
Shade of His hand, outstretched caressingly?
 "Ah, fondest, blindest, weakest,
 I am He Whom thou seekest!
Thou dravest love from thee, who dravest Me."

from *Masterpieces of Religious Verse*,
edited by James Dalton Morrison, pp. 57–61.

PART TWO

Connecting:
What Is the Soul?

Chapter 6

FINDING GOD'S THUMBPRINT

Is there any word out there for the victims of the soul-eaters, prey of the spiritual cannibals so omnipresent these days? Is there a message of hope to be spoken into the moral vacuum that seems to be sucking society under?

Sam Keen isn't very optimistic. In his *Fire in the Belly,* Keen says, "With the postmodern man we reach a point where moral reasoning gives out. Once we abandon the age-old quest for consistency, for forging a single identity, for a unifying vision we are left with no guiding principle except to follow the dictates of the moment."[1]

No consolation there; only confirmation of our fears.

And yet there is a surprise. Lack of direction has sent many disillusioned contemporaries back to ancient sources for a more profound source of encouragement, and no book has greater antiquity than *The Holy Bible.* Rediscovery of the Scripture has always resulted in the recovery of direction, purpose, and moral certainty. Today multitudes are turning again to what the Bible and centuries of Christian experience reveal about finding our lost souls.

Since only the Creator can fully explain the creation, revelation is the singular hope for ultimate insight into this mysterious entity so crucial for our humanity. We turn in this chapter to the Old Testament story of two thousand years of searching for the soul. In the next chapter, we investigate how the coming of the Christ was a spiritual compass for the quest. The three subsequent chapters are the insights of the church fathers who explored and expanded upon the teachings of the apostles.

The Holy Bible and Christian tradition have been for twenty centuries the beacon lights along the shore leading us on through dark and foggy nights of confusion. Scripture describes itself as a "lamp unto our feet." No source could be more helpful and reassuring to us in understanding the soul.

If . . . if we can figure out what it means.

In the next two chapters, we are going to depart from the format of the rest of the book in order to understand what the scriptures tell us. Scripture passages along with commentary lets us put one foot in the ancient world while keeping the other foot in our time. Modern parallels from contemporary experience serve as a wall off of which to bounce our thoughts and condition our feelings.

The trip can't be all in our head or the journey will fail. Issues of the heart, threats of survival, soul-wrenching agonies are necessary if we are finally to find our own soul. We must listen to the cries of our fellow travelers to the grave if we are to understand.

In this sea of troubled souls in which we daily swim, we need a lifeline. Let's look again for the guiding principles and unifying identity we so desperately seek today.

Can we find a point of contact and once again touch the hand of God?

And God Breathed

Where does the human story start? What makes us different from the animals? God breathed a soul into Homo sapiens and history began:

> This is the account of the heavens and the earth when they were created in the day that the Lord God made heaven and earth. Now no shrub of the field was yet in the earth, and no plant of the field had yet sprouted, for the Lord God had not sent rain upon the earth; and there was no man to cultivate the ground. But a mist used to rise from the earth and water the whole surface of the ground. Then the Lord God formed man of dust from the ground, and breathed into his nostril the breath of life, and man became a living being.
>
> Genesis 2:4b–7

Animals were created but not breathed upon. The Hebrew words for soul and breath are essentially synonymous. We owe our being and uniqueness to existence in a God-permeated atmosphere.

Like the natural atmosphere in which we live, the breath of God fills us, sustains us, surrounds us, and maintains our existence. As one would have a hard time explaining water to a goldfish, so the breath of God is both unavoidably obvious and a complete mystery.

The Old Testament defines personality in these terms. A person is literally a living soul.

He took his wife Sarai, his nephew Lot, all the
possessions they had accumulated and the people they
had acquired in Haran, and they set out for the land of
Canaan, and they arrived there.

Genesis 12:5, NIV

The Old Testament story suggests we go on living
when we lose our sense of God's having breathed life into
us, but our uniqueness disappears. Animal dimensions gain
ascendance over the original purposes of God. We stand
on the threshold of the death of our humanity.

Life in the Blood

Every moving thing that is alive shall be food for you; I
give you all to you, as I gave the green plant. Only you
shall not eat flesh with its life, that is, its blood. And
surely I will require your lifeblood; from every beast I
will require it. And from every man, from every man's
brother I will require the life of man. Whoever sheds
man's blood, by man his blood shall be shed, For in the
image of God He made man.

Genesis 9:3–6

The Old Testament described life and the soul as being
intricately involved with the bloodstream. Similar to the loss
of breath, as blood drains away, so the soul departs and
vitality is gone. Because of this relationship, the Old Testament developed an elaborate sacrificial system to ensure
forgiveness of sin and the restoration of vitality to the soul.

The book of Leviticus prescribed animal sacrifice to
restore humanness to God's errant people. The Hebrew
people believed any action that separated the person from
a vital relationship with God was tantamount to death.

Subsequently, offering of life was required to counteract the death of the soul. Consequently the Temple worship system was the means by which personal restoration was achieved.

> For the life of the flesh is in the blood, and I have given it to you upon the altar to make atonement for your souls; for it is the blood that makes atonement for the soul.
>
> Leviticus 17:11

The Old Testament foresaw the need for a suffering servant to rise out of Israel. Through his own pain, this servant would fully accomplish the redemption of lost souls, returning them to the fulfilled relationship with God intended by him. The suffering servant would complete what was lacking in animal sacrifice.

> Therefore, I will allot Him a portion with the great, And He will divide the booty with the strong; Because He poured out Himself to the death, And was numbered with the transgressors; Yet He Himself bore the sin of many, And interceded for the transgressors.
>
> Isaiah 53:12b

If the loss of the soul equals death, is it any surprise that we are living today in what is often called "a culture of death"? Without a means of restoration of the soul, the ambiance of life continues to evaporate.

Locating the Soul

With cannibals lurking on our TV screens and soul massacres reported daily on the six o'clock news, we desperately need to get in touch with our own losses. Just exactly where does one find the soul? In the bloodstream? A special pocket in the brain? Is the soul distributed throughout the body? Could we find a place where a surgeon could cut with a knife? A researcher place electrodes? Because our age looks to science for ultimate answers, we assume anything that is real must have a location.

What hints does the Old Testament give us? Can the stories of the Bible pinpoint the seat of the soul?

Let's examine the text. Sometimes the Scripture sounds as if the soul is linked to the place of passion.

> And he was deeply attracted to Dinah the daughter of Jacob, and he loved the girl and spoke tenderly to her. . . . But Hamor spoke with them, saying, "The soul of my son Shechem longs for your daughter; please give her to him in marriage."
>
> Genesis 34:3, 8

In this passage, the suggestion seems to be that the soul is linked to human desire. Another view is that the soul is a part of the affections, much like the heart is used symbolically on Valentine's Day.

However, in other passages the soul seems to have something to do with willpower. We might wonder if our ability to be intentional is what the soul is about. Look at this passage describing an imminent attack.

> Moreover David was greatly distressed because the people spoke of stoning him, for all the people were bitter in soul, each one because of his sons and his daughters.
>
> 1 Samuel 30:6

On the other hand, other passages sound as if the soul is connected with sorrow and sadness.

> Also they will make themselves bald for you. And gird themselves with sackcloth; And they will weep for you in bitterness of soul.
>
> Ezekiel 27:31

> Job said, As surely as God lives, who has denied my justice, the Almighty, who has made me taste bitterness of soul, as long as I have life within me, the breath of God in my nostrils, my lips will not speak wickedness, and my tongue will utter no deceit.
>
> Job 27:1–4

Sometimes the head seems to be the command station for the soul. The book of Daniel speaks of dreams arising from the soul and "passing through the mind."[2] The blessing from father to firstborn son is given by putting hands on the head to connect with the soul.

On the other hand, the heart appears more often to be the center of life. The Psalmist often cries out for the Lord to examine the heart and mind in an effort to find restoration of the soul.[3]

In Hebrew worship, unique symbolic ornaments were worn to call attention to the special place the heart had in approaching God. The chest piece had a jewel for every tribe in Israel. The Lord instructed:

> And Aaron shall carry the names of the sons of Israel in the breastpiece of judgment over his heart when he enters the holy place, for a memorial before the Lord continually. And he shall put in the breastpiece of judgment the Urim and Thummim, and they shall be

over Aaron's heart when he goes in before the Lord;
and Aaron shall carry the judgment of the sons of Israel
over his heart before the Lord continually.

Exodus 28:29–30

The unusual object offers us a clue as to what was going on in Hebrew minds. In a prepsychological age, the heart was used to express the personal dynamics of emotion and motivation. Pain and joy, happiness and despair arise and coalesce in the heart. The totality of the experience of life was represented by the heart. The Old Testament suggests both memory and conscience are also found in the heart.

These verses and a host of other passages leave us with the impression that the location of the soul moves around inside us. As we look for locale, the terrain only shifts and becomes more mysterious. The Old Testament leaves us with quandary and indecision. Location is not exact.

So let's try another door. Could the Old Testament have been describing a function rather than a place? Could suggestions of location be used metaphorically? When Hamor said his soul longed for Dinah, his expression was of passion. Aaron's breastplate over his heart was symbolic. Might the soul express itself from time to time more forcefully by coming from different places on the human landscape?

Because Hebrew language is unusually concrete, word pictures are generally used to suggest abstract concepts. Rather than saying the Jews were stubborn, Scripture says "they were a stiff-necked people." Consequently, we might consider a different perspective on talk about body parts and places. *The Bible isn't as concerned with place as with function.*

And Who Cares?

What difference does it make to us what people living three thousand years ago thought? Why should we care if the Old Testament links vitality to breath and blood? What difference does it make where the soul is found?

Why? Because we want to know where we can find a new dose of life, a "shot" of reassurance.

The music of blues musician Robert Johnson asks the same questions about location. The longing sound of his music expressed a yearning to find a lost soul. Arising out of the despair, dejection, and emptiness of life on the Mississippi Delta, the passion of his music was a quest for answers to a desperate inquiry about life, hope, and purpose.

Greil Marcus observes,

Blues grew out of the need to live in the brutal world that stood ready in ambush the moment one walked out of the church. Unlike gospel, blues was not a music of transcendence; its equivalent to God's Grace was sex and love. Blues made the terrors of the world easier to endure, but blues also made those terrors more real. For a man like Johnson, the promises of the church faded; they could be remembered—as one sang church songs; perhaps even when one prayed, when one was scared not to—but those promises could not be live. Once past some unmarked border, one could not go back. The weight of Johnson's blues was strong enough to make salvation a joke; the best he could do was cry for its beautiful life. "You run without moving from the terror in which you cannot believe," William Faulkner wrote in one of his books about the landscape he

shared with Robert Johnson, just about the time
Johnson was making his first record, "toward a safety
in which you have no faith."[4]

Heavy breathing and hot blood are what the songs of
Johnson were all about, and he was convinced soul was
still to be found there. Blues is certainly as primitive as the
Hebrews in the desert, but the issue isn't antiquity, it's life.

When we look at the Old Testament prophets and
psalmists through the end of a trumpet, a number of things
come into perspective. The issue isn't anthropology but
passion, not religious form but capacity to go in the face
of overwhelming odds.

Moses, Robert Johnson, and William Faulkner wanted
to know if God is in there someplace. Johnson and Faulkner gave up on God; Moses insisted God won't give up
on us.

In this sense, we get a new twist from what old agonizing Jeremiah was about. The recovery of one's soul begins
when the heart turns back to God.

"For I know the plans that I have for you," declares the
Lord, "plans for welfare and not for calamity to give
you a future and a hope. Then you will call upon Me,
and I will listen to you. And you will seek Me and find
Me, when you search for Me with all your heart. And I
will be found by you," declares the Lord, "and I will
restore your fortunes."

Jeremiah 29:11–14a

Let us push on with the sounds of Robert Johnson's
guitar playing in the background and the haunting pain of
his music hanging in the air to see if there is some answer

for people who aren't sure the promises of the church can be lived out.

The Wellspring of Hope

Here is a sample of the Old Testament's response to the need for a little soul music.

Hear my prayer, O Lord; let my cry for help come to you; Do not hide your face from me when I am in distress. Turn your ear to me; when I call, answer me quickly. For my days vanish like smoke; my bones burn like glowing embers; My heart is blighted and withered like grass; I forget to eat my food.

                                                    Psalm 102:1–2

Vindicate me, O LORD, For I have walked in my integrity; I have also trusted in the LORD; I shall not slip.

                                                    Psalm 26:1–2

O God, hasten to deliver me; O LORD, hasten to my help! Let those be ashamed and humiliated who seek my life; Let those be turned back and dishonored who delight in my hurt. Let those be turned back because of their shame who say "aha, aha"!

                                                    Psalm 70:1–2

The inner worth of the soul is expressed by the heart. Nothing abstract here, the cry arises from the slave huts on the banks of the Nile . . . and the same shacks on the Mississippi's muddy banks. And the answer comes back:

Many are the afflictions of the righteous, but the LORD delivers him out of them all. He guards all his bones; not one of them is broken.

Psalm 34:19–29

Do not fret because of evildoers. Be not be envious toward wrongdoers. For they will wither quickly like the grass, and fade like the green herb. Trust in the LORD, and do good. . . . Rest in the LORD and wait patiently for Him.

Psalm 37:1–3, 7

Behold, the eye of the LORD is on those who fear Him, on those who hope for his lovingkindness, to deliver their soul from death, and to keep them alive in famine.

Psalm 33:18–19

Soul food, indeed! Therefore, let's return to the Hebrew perspective again. What hope is there for people when the soul has been gobbled up by conflict and desperation? How do we get back in touch?

When God Breathes Again

The Creator, the lover of our soul, flies through the heavens: David sang to the LORD the words of this song when the LORD delivered him from the hand of all his enemies and from the hand of Saul; In my distress I called to the LORD; I called out to my God. From his temple he heard my voice; my cry came to his ears; He mounted the cherubim and flew; he soared on the wings of the wind.

2 Samuel 22:1, 7, 11

Scripture paints a word picture of the Spirit of God sweeping across the globe like the coming of a mighty tempest. Nothing can stand against his coming.

> So Moses stretched out his staff over Egypt, and the LORD made an east wind blow across the land all that day and all that night. By morning the wind had brought the locust.
>
> Exodus 10:14

> Now the earth was formless and empty, darkness was over the face of the deep, and the Spirit of God [could be translated "mighty wind"] was hovering over the waters.
>
> Genesis 1:2

We are able to get in touch again if we know and remember that as the blowing wind brings change, so the Spirit of God returns again and again to creation, surging through his people bringing change. We have to stand where the wind is blowing.

The Spirit of God revitalizes depleted souls. The breath of God can return vitality and rejuvenation to his people.

> These all look to you to give them their food at the proper time; when you give it to them, they gather it up; when you open your hand, they are satisfied with good things. When you hide your face, they are terrified. when you take away their breath, they die and return to the dust; When you send your Spirit, they are created, and you renew the face of the earth.
>
> Psalm 104:27–30

Even when Israel was thoroughly corrupt and rightly set aside from her mission. God did not leave his people to suffocate in their iniquity.

> This is what God the LORD says . . . He who created the heavens and stretched them out, who spread out the earth and all that comes out of it, who gives breath to its people, and life to those who walk on it: I, the LORD, have called you in righteousness; I will take hold of your hand. I will keep you and will make you to be a covenant for the people and a light for the Gentiles.
>
> Isaiah 42:5–6

Once the breath of God returns, life follows. Both individuals and nations are reborn.

Destiny Recovered

Reconnected to the Spirit of God, lost souls discover they have power and capacity beyond anything they could have dreamed. The restoration of soul is more than a recovery of connectedness. Significant strength, ability to achieve, guidance, and awareness are imparted. Remember the story of Samson?

> Then the woman gave birth to a son and named him Samson; and the child grew up and the LORD blessed him. And the Spirit of the LORD began to stir him in Mahaned-dan, between Zorah and Eshtaol.
>
> Judges 13:24–25

> Then Samson went down to Timnah with his father and mother and came as far as the vineyards of Timnah. And behold a young lion came roaring toward

him. And the Spirit of the LORD came upon him
mightily, so that he tore him as one tears a kid though
he had nothing in his hand.

Judges 14:5–6

When he came to Lehi, the Philistines shouted as they
met him. And the Spirit of the LORD came upon him
so mightily so that the ropes that were on his arms
were as flax that is burned with fire, and his bonds
dropped from his hands. And he found a fresh jawbone
of a donkey, so he reached out and took it and killed a
thousand men with it.

Judges 15:14–15

When the young man Saul was anointed by Samuel
to be king over Israel, he also received the promise of
empowerment.

Then the Spirit of the LORD will come upon you
mightily, and you shall prophesy with them and be
changed into another man. And it shall be when these
signs come to you, do for yourself what the occasion
requires; for God is with you.

1 Samuel 10:6–7

When the breath of God is moving, inspiration spills
over in unexpected ways. Indeed, as the prophecy to Saul
was fulfilled, a similar experience came to David when he
was being pursued by Saul. The very soldiers sent to cap-
ture David were turned into prophets. Bystanders found
their souls were equally empowered.

Then Saul sent messengers to take David, but when
they saw the company of the prophets prophesying,

with Samuel standing and presiding over them, the Spirit of God came upon the messengers of Saul; and they also prophesied. And when it was told Saul, he sent other messengers, and they also prophesied. So Saul sent messengers again the third time, and they also prophesied.

1 Samuel 19:20–21

Something of great significance is happening in each of these stories. When God breathes, new life and possibility follow. People become more than they were before.

No joking about salvation here. Far from "pie-in-the-sky and by-and-by," the Old Testament stories of soul recovery are amazing affirmations of human potential.

Why so?

The Image Dei

Our question will lead us to one of our most significant insights the Old Testament offers on the meaning of the soul. As has been implied, the Hebrew writers perceived the soul to be a function more than a place. In an even larger sense, the *nephesh,* the soul, is not something we possess as much as a summing up of our total nature. Scripture suggests the soul is like a mirror held before the face of God reflecting his image.

Loss of soul obscures our ability to "look like" our heavenly Papa, our Creator. Recovery of the soul restores the Image Dei in us. Writers of Scripture recognize how crucial recovery is.

O God, Thou art my God; I shall seek Thee earnestly;
My soul thirsts for Thee, my flesh years for Thee, In a

dry and weary land where there is no water. Thus I
have beheld Thee in the sanctuary, to see Thy power
and Thy glory. Because Thy lovingkindness is better
than life, My lips will praise Thee. So I will bless Thee
as long as I live; I will lift up my hands in Thy name.
My soul is satisfied as with marrow and fatness. And
my mouth offers praises with joyful lips.

Psalm 63:1–5

I wait for the LORD, my soul does wait, And in His
word do I hope. My soul waits for the LORD; More
than the watchmen for the morning; Indeed, more than
the watchmen for the morning. O Israel hope in the
LORD, For with the LORD there is lovingkindness,
And with Him is abundant redemption.

Psalm 130:5–6

These passages suggest that the proper study of hu-
mankind is not anthropology as much as theology. Not
by looking at ourselves but by pursuing God do we find
out who we are meant to be. Recovery of perspective
grants us powers beyond anything we dreamed possible.

The Image of God is his thumbprint on our lives. The
closest the modern age has come to this inspired concept
is the idea of the ego. However, the Old Testament's sense
of personal unity still eludes our time. Today we are considered as a conscience, a superego, an id, a personality.
The Hebrews knew nothing of dividing us up into pieces
of personality, into body and soul or even body, soul, and
spirit. Humanity before God has a singular unity and can
only be understood as a totality, because this is the way
God is.

We stand before God as a homogeneity. Spirit, heart, and flesh are encompassed and included in the soul. The soul is both the center and circumference of our existence.

When all the aspects of what we call personality combine in a singular quest for God, the recovery of soul has begun and human beings reach their potential and ability. Once the quest for the soul is fulfilled, human beings are completely and totally fulfilled. We can rest in the palm of the hand that creates us.

Let's put it in terms of the terrain where Robert Johnson and William Faulkner would feel most comfortable. Gert Behanna knew those backwoods exceedingly well. After her recovery from a life of alcoholism, she wrote her autobiography under the pen name of Elizabeth Burns. In *The Late Liz, The Autobiography of an Ex-Pagan,* Gert gives us a Hebrew view of rebirth. She begins chapter 1,

> Death isn't so cut and dried as it sounds. In looking back I see now that my life is a series of small deaths. For example, some of me died when, very young, I accepted the fact that my father hated my mother. Some of me died each time I sat on the side lines wondering what secret you had to know to get the boys to dance with you. And then a great chunk of me died at the first night of my first marriage. After that, it was death after death.[5]

Gert was a dear friend who helped me find my soul. She could do so because of her remarkable ability to reflect the Imago Dei. After twenty-four chapters of describing her journey from debauchery to divinity, Gert ends the story with this description of what it is like to be redefined by the love of God.

This is my life today and I would not have it otherwise only more so. I know freedom from stuff in bottles, from guilt and fear and resentment and material possessions, from the judgment of human beings, myself included. My days are filled with challenge and almost too much drama, but, above all, I am at peace with myself. The only Judge I have to make a hit with is the Judge of judges.[6]

Countless thousands were blessed by the Great Gert, who spent the rest of her life telling the story of her recovery and helping multitudes find theirs.

Perhaps the leap from the ancient world to ours is not as great as it seems. Clearly, God is still breathing and souls are coming back to life.

Chapter 7

LIFE
ABUNDANTLY

The first century's search for the soul provides us with a lofty vantage point. Everything described in the last chapter stands as the backdrop, the great panorama against which the new story unfolds.

The ancient longing for the Messiah came to full fruition in Jesus of Nazareth as the new seekers stood on the shoulders of prophets, priests, and kings to see this new thing God had done. And the matter is very much about the soul.

One cannot but notice that immediately following the grand announcement to Mary of a most unexpected child, she exclaims:

My soul exalts the Lord, And my spirit has rejoiced in God my Savior. For he has had regard for the humble state of bondslave: For behold, from this time on all generations will count me blessed. For the Might One has gone great things for me; And Holy is His name.

Luke 1:46–47

But the proper place to begin this story is not with Mary's joy at the exaltation of her own soul as much as with the squalor and poverty of the times, the pain and injustice of everyday life. Jesus was the son of a captive people daily annihilated at the whim of their brutal masters. He came as light into a very dark age.

The paintings of Rembrandt and Master Raphael aside, Jesus was not born in a cathedral beneath priceless stained glass. While his world was filled with crosses, none were gold. All were covered with the corpora of countrymen unceremoniously hung out to dry for simply being Jews at the wrong time and place in history. Truly an age of lost souls!

Perhaps we get a better feel of the problem by looking to a contemporary Jewish scene strangely analogous to the slaughter of the infants Matthew records in the second chapter of his Gospel. In the novel *Sophie's Choice,* William Styron states, "I seek the essential region of the soul where absolute evil confronts brotherhood."[1] Styron's narrator, the budding young writer Stingo, befriends a distraught and helpless refugee. He exposes to us the darkest side of the soul by introducing Nathan Landau and his captive paramour, Sophie.

Sophie is an immigrant and displaced person, driftwood washed ashore by World War II. She is a woman of mystery. As if some foreboding secret lurks just behind one of the smoking crematoriums, Sophie's story of her sojourn in Auschwitz is never quite complete.

Stingo is intrigued by Sophie's total preoccupation with guilt, a faceless, relentless guilt present in every aspect of her life. Stingo concludes that the woman is absorbed in self-loathing.

To describe her condition, Styron quotes the Christian writer Simone Weil. "Affliction stamps the soul to its very depths with the scorn, the disgust and even the self-hatred and sense of guilt that crime logically should produce but actually does not." Sophie has stood before a tribunal in her own soul and been found guilty. She exists in a living sentence of death.

At the height of the story, we discover why. When Sophie entered Auschwitz death camp, the Nazis forced her to choose which of her two children would live. In order to save one, she had to sacrifice the other. An innocent victim of all-encompassing evil, Sophie's gnarled and bent existence continues as a perpetual extension of the death camp.

With the smell of smoke in our nostrils and the cries of dispossessed victims like Sophie ringing in our ears, we are better prepared to read of the new soul search that begins in A.D. 33, as Jesus comes speaking of a peace this world can never give. The Scripture claims he came to descend into the depths of guilt to once again ascend and set us free. We are also in the region of the soul where absolute temptation meets redemption.

The Soul Man Cometh

The Old Testament idea of God had been like a picture frame around the universe. The portrait of Jesus of Nazareth within that frame put a comprehensible face on the Creator. As Jesus fulfilled the centuries-old hope and promise of a Messiah, he became the picture of what God truly is and a human being can be. In the person of Jesus of Nazareth, time and eternity, humanity and divinity were united and joined never to be separated. Because Jesus spoke and taught about the soul, the subject became of paramount importance to the church.

The record is clear. Eyewitnesses proclaimed with enthusiasm and awe, "God was in Christ reconciling the world unto himself." Completed and fulfilled in Jesus Christ, God's self-disclosure also enlarged their understanding of the human soul.

Jesus Christ was Lord over law, sin, and even death. The demons shuddered and scattered at his word; captives of evil were set free and the blind had sight restored. He spoke directly to the aspirations and hopes of men and women as one knowing intimately the depths of the soul. Jesus proclaimed, "I have come that they might have life and have it abundantly." He clearly had the capacity to revitalize and heal the soul.

The Sophies and Nathans of our time desperately want to know if the story is really true. And if so, how can they find the promise?

Much to our consolation, the New Testament is filled with important insight and guidance for recovering and understanding the soul. For an account of divine revelation, we eagerly turn to that remarkable story of when the soul of God and humanity met and joined in Bethlehem. We read to see if it is still possible for divinity to meet and connect again with our souls in an equally wicked world.

The True Center of Life

Jesus' teaching consistently used the word *soul* for life. In both Matthew's and Mark's gospels, *soul* was used as a synonym for physical life. In contrast to what people might think, sacrifice, not self-indulgence, is the path to fulfillment.

Then he called the crowd to him along with his disciples and said: "If anyone would come after me, he must deny himself and take up his cross and follow me. For whoever wants to save his life will lose it, but whoever loses his life for me and for the gospel will save it. What good is it for a man to gain the whole world, yet forfeit his soul? Or what can a man give in exchange for his soul?

Mark 8:34–37 NIV

Genuine existence is more than simply being alive. The "good life" is not enough to give our time on earth enduring meaning. Affluence is a poor substitute for significance. Health and wealth crumble in the face of death.

The recovery of the soul through the Christ is the only path to fullness, direction, and hope—in short, to life. Jesus said:

"I am the door; if anyone enters through Me, he shall be saved, and shall go in and out, and find pasture. The thief comes only to steal and kill and destroy; I have come that they might have life, and have it abundantly. I am the good shepherd. The good shepherd lays down his life for the sheep."

John 10:9–11

New life in Christ has more than temporal significance. A vital force is released that can be found nowhere else. Eternal life is not automatically resident in the soul itself but must come from God.

Now this is eternal life: that they may know you, the only true God, and Jesus Christ, whom you have sent.

John 17:3

Jesus tells us a paradoxical and surprising thing about the quest to find our soul.

> "Anyone who loves his father or mother more than me is not worthy of me; anyone who loves his son or daughter more than me is not worthy of me; and anyone who does not take his cross and follow me is not worthy of me. Whoever finds his life will lose it, and whoever loses his life for my sake will find it. He who receives you receives me, and he who receives me receives the one who sent me."
>
> Matthew 10:37–40

Only when we are completely ready to lose our lives (our souls) and confront what seems to be certain death, do we actually find ourselves. Only there can the surrendered life or soul truly encounter God, the Father and Creator.

Eternal Life

In contrast to the ideas of Plato and the Greek world, the soul was not simply a permanent possession, which humanity automatically carried forward after death. Only through one's relationship to the Christ is there an assurance of immortality.

> "Truly, truly I say to you, unless a grain of wheat falls into the earth and dies, it remains by itself alone; But if it dies, it bears much fruit. He who loves his life loses it, and he who hates his life in this world will keep it for life eternal. If anyone serve me, let him follow Me;

and where I am, there shall my servant also be. The Father will honor him."

John 12:24–26

Jesus tells his disciples he alone is going to pioneer the way to eternity for them. Of course, they cannot grasp this idea until after they see Jesus on the cross, which he foretold in this passage. However, this way of sacrifice applied to them as well. The disciples had to discover the center of true life! The point of life-giving contact for the soul was found along the path of self-denial ending at the feet of Jesus Christ.

In all of these passages, Jesus Christ brings fullness of life *now*. At his touch, the soul is renewed and life is extended into eternity. In contrast to the Greek idea of body and soul separating at death, Jesus promised a fullness of life *today*. The life Jesus brought was for the here and now, not just the there and then. Fulfillment begins at the moment the soul is recovered.

Jesus did not just speak of life in another world. Those who have lost their souls are already dead. On the other hand, the recovery of the soul produces a life that never stops. True affluence is not accumulation of possessions; rather, possession of one's soul is imperishable wealth. No one can take this pearl of great price from us.

The Victory That Overcomes the World

Will the usual scene at the average church on Sunday morning give us a full understanding of the difference Jesus made for the dispossessed souls of his time? We struggle with such overpowering issues as whether this year we must settle for the Toyota rather than the BMW or Lincoln.

We wrestle with rising health care costs, not the fact that untreatable infection will inevitably lead to amputation and probably death. The average church member is praying to prosper, not survive.

Again we must look to a more critical life-and-death moment to grasp the power of redemption and perseverance offered through the ministry of Jesus of Nazareth. Generally our mundane problems don't draw deeply enough on the wealth of empowerment he brought to the soul to reveal the potential that is ours in Christ.

For an image and a parable of what the teaching of Jesus promises today, we might return to Auschwitz and a story of another choice.

The first time I visited Auschwitz, it was near the end of January. Even the sun looked frozen in the gray sky. Wind and freezing humidity turned the unbearable temperatures into a thousand ice picks that poked though anything I wore. Even though I was well prepared for the winter day, my toes still ached and my fingertips burned. The subfreezing temperatures were almost impossible to endure.

The death camp has been well preserved, and most of the buildings are as the Nazis left them. The crematoriums look almost ready for use again; the showers for gassing unsuspecting victims are just as they were when the last Jews crumpled to the floor.

Several of the dormitories have been turned into museums. Piles of marked bags and luggage against one wall are stacked as if their owners will return to pick them up before leaving. On the opposite side of the room, empty green cans of cyclone-B gas remind us they won't.

Another room is divided by a sheet of glass holding back an avalanche of piles of human hair clipped from

Jewish bodies. At one end behind the glass exhibit are several bolts of cloth on display. The Nazis, experimenting with possible uses of the tons of hair, had made the material from the locks of the dead.

I stood out on the open assembly ground at the exact place the prisoners assembled each day, and tried to feel what winter mornings on this spot must have been like. With my fur hat and sheepskin coat on, I had far too much insulation to get an accurate idea. I took the heavy overcoat off. In a matter of seconds, I wondered how anyone *ever* survived.

Just a few feet away is Father Maximilian Kolbe's cell.

On one of those torturous mornings, someone had escaped. In order to instill absolute fear, prisoners would be executed to demonstrate the penalty for failure to submit totally to Nazi rule. When the scapegoat was yanked from the line, the man begged for mercy. He had a wife, children, responsibilities; but the plea meant nothing to his captors. His death would prove their point.

Maximilian Kolbe was forty-five years old when he entered Auschwitz for the crime of publishing unapproved material. The SS told him the life expectancy of a priest in the camp was one month. The priest had endured under impossible circumstances.

To the amazement of the assembly of guards and captives, Father Kolbe stepped forward as the pleading prisoner was being prepared for death in a torture cell. The Roman Catholic priest was celibate, no children in his house. He offered himself in exchange.

Death didn't follow at the execution wall where so many were shot each week. Father Kolbe was returned to an isolation cell to have the life slowly squeezed out of him. Prisoners were left to fade away in agony without water or food. To the consternation of the guards, courage and perseverance oozed through his pores. He prayed, sang, and recited the Breviary. Father Kolbe died with a smile on his face, his eyes open and fixed on some distant vision. Observers were left with the distinct impression that Father Kolbe, not his tormentors, was in control.

Five decades later, the priest is not remembered so much for the overwhelming pain he endured as for the sense of life he exemplified. He endures as a symbol that once Jesus Christ imparts life to a person, courage, valor, virtuousness, and magnanimity follow. Such development of personhood is life indeed!

When Death Comes Early

Jesus' teaching of life was always proclaimed in the face of death. Men did well to get beyond their thirties; every family left a child buried somewhere. In an age long before the development of anesthesia and antiseptics, penicillin and X-rays, there was a natural urgency to know if the soul was going anywhere. The multitudes gladly heard the prophet from Nazareth.

As goldfish have no idea what water is, people simply accept life as their natural condition of existence. Perspective is lost on what we have until the time comes when the meaning of life is gone. Jesus warns that at that point of awareness we are already dead. Like fish happily swimming in contaminated waters, the clarity of the blue water is only illusion. Death floats at our side disguised as normalcy.

Judgment is inevitable. The future of our situation depends on how we publicly relate to Jesus Christ. Final judgment will only reveal the judgments happening every day. These moments of truth expose the soul and its true condition. What emerges is not a "something," which floats away from the body at death, but the bearer of life itself. The deepest truth about who we are will be eternally displayed.

Actually, people do not have the capacity to control life or existence. In a theological sense, no one takes his own life. Suicide simply terminates this mode of existence. God alone takes and gives life. Having a soul offers no guarantees.

> So do not be afraid of them. There is nothing concealed that will not be disclosed, or hidden that will not be made known. What I tell you in the dark, speak in the daylight; what is whispered in your ear, proclaim from the roofs. Do not be afraid of those who kill the body but cannot kill the soul. Rather, be afraid of the One [God] who can destroy both soul and body in hell.
>
> Matthew 10:26–28, NIV

Jesus did not believe in the idea of the immortality of the soul as taught by Plato. The soul has no such independence as if it were by itself a force to be reckoned with. Every living thing is subject to and under the sovereignty of God. Only God can take and give life. Death is merely a point of transition along the way as the soul, the bearer of life, moves toward either fulfillment or destruction as God alone decides.

People foolishly believe life is their own to do with as they please. Aren't we the captains of our fate? The masters of our own destinies? Jesus taught that such arrogance leads to the loss of soul and death. To the contrary, we are only stewards of the gift of life. At any given moment, an accounting of this precious loan may be required. At such a point, life and soul are basically synonymous.

> And He told them a parable saying, "The land of a certain rich man was very productive. And he began reasoning to himself, saying, What shall I do, since I have no place to store my crops?" And he said, "This is what I will do: I will tear down my barns and build larger ones, and there I will store all my grain and my goods. And I will say to my soul, 'Soul, you have many goods laid up for many years to come, take your ease, eat, drink and be merry.'"
>
> But God said to him, "You fool! This very night your soul is required of you; and now who will own what you have prepared?"
>
> So is the man who lays up treasure for himself, and is not rich toward God.
>
> Luke 12:16–21

To Look Death in the Eye

What does it mean to come to the moment when one confronts the hard, cold reality of personal mortality? How does it feel to rub hands and press the flesh with the grim reaper? The New Testament offers us a cross. The modern world has other forms of agonizing death to make the same point. Elie Wiesel offers a view of the grave from his own reflections on life in the death camp at the edge of eternity.

Wiesel was but a boy when his family was deported from Hungary to Auschwitz and later on to Buchenwald. His parents and sister never returned. His classic remembrances, *Night,* won the 1986 Nobel Peace Prize. The final pages of the book describe the last days before liberation and his release. Ironically, three days later Elie ate bad food and ended up with food poisoning that nearly finished him off.

After days of agony in a hospital, the survivor was able to get on his feet and peer into a mirror. He had not seen his reflection since leaving the ghetto. Wiesel wrote, "I wanted to see myself in the mirror hanging on the opposite wall. I had not seen myself since the ghetto. From the depths of the mirror, a corpse gazed back at me. The look in his eyes, as they stared into mine, has never left me."[2]

Perhaps, such a moment of insight is necessary to understand the truth about our very limited and fragile existence.

And with What Shape Do They Come Forth?

What does Jesus tell us is the hereafter of the soul? As new life permeates us, what form does our future existence take? To the Greek's hope of immortality, Jesus said, "No." Instead, the Master promised physical resurrection.

Luke clearly wrote to a Greek audience. He wanted the followers of Plato to correct the misconceptions of the great teacher. Luke's Gospel, generally considered to be written later in the first century, carefully made his point with a clever literary device. Do you see what is missing in the following passages from what you read earlier?

"I tell you, my friends, do not be afraid of those who kill the body and after that can do no more. But I will show you whom you should fear: Fear him who, after the killing of the body, has power to throw you into hell. Yes, I tell you, fear him. . . ."

Then he said to them all: "If anyone would come after me, he must deny himself and take up his cross daily and follow me. For whoever wants to save his life will lose it, but whoever loses his life for me will save it. What good is it for a man to gain the whole world, and yet lose or forfeit his very self? If anyone is ashamed of me and my words, the Son of Man will be ashamed of him when he comes in his glory and in the glory of the Father and of the holy angels."

Luke 12:4–5; Luke 9:23–26, NIV

See what's left out? Matthew's earlier allusions to body and soul have been trimmed away. Luke doesn't want the Greeks to misconstrue Jesus' teaching to mean a soul is going to be punished after death once the body is jettisoned. Notice what he says in Acts:

Seeing what was ahead, he spoke of the resurrection of the Christ, that he was not abandoned to the grave, nor did his body see decay.

Acts 2:31, NIV

He avoids any idea of a soul being left in Hades by returning our attention to the bodily resurrection of Jesus.

Luke is particularly concerned to demonstrate that the Easter story is an account of a resurrected body. Earlier in his Gospel, he described an afterlife episode, putting great emphasis on bodily appearance and shape.

"There was a rich man who was dressed in purple and fine linen and lived in luxury every day. At his gate was laid a beggar named Lazarus, covered with sores and longing to eat what fell from the rich man's table. Even the dogs came and licked his sores.

"The time came when the beggar died and the angels carried him to Abraham's side. The rich man also died and was buried. In hell, where he was in torment, he looked up and saw Abraham far away, with Lazarus by his side. So he called to him, 'Father Abraham, have pity on me and send Lazarus to dip the tip of his finger in water and cool my tongue, because I am in agony in this fire.'

"But Abraham replied, 'Son, remember that in your lifetime you received your good things, while Lazarus received bad things, but now he is comforted here and you are in agony. And besides all this, between us and you a great chasm has been fixed, so that those who want to go from here to you cannot, nor can anyone cross over from there to us.'

"He answered, 'Then I beg you, father, send Lazarus to my father's house, for I have five brothers. Let him warn them, so that they will not also come to this place of torment.'

"Abraham replied, 'They have Moses and the Prophets; let them listen to them.'

"'No, father Abraham,' he said, 'but if someone from the dead goes to them, they will repent.'

"He said to him, 'If they do not listen to Moses and the Prophets, they will not be convinced even if someone rises from the dead.'"

Luke 16:19–31, NIV

No ghoulish "Casper the friendly ghost" floating around there! The tormented face judgment with hands, feet, eyes, and ears! The soul can't be siphoned off and extracted from what makes people human.

Tomorrow Redefined

The rest of the New Testament builds on this idea of the soul as the bearer of true life. The apostle Paul often used the word *soul* to designate man as a whole, a person or an individual. As a Jew with a foot planted in the Greek world, Paul obviously knew the implications of what he was writing. He had gone through the ancient world proclaiming new life in Christ. Paul wanted the new believers to know that conversion of the soul renews one's life.

> Therefore from now on we regard no man according to the flesh. Even though we have known Christ according to the flesh; yet now we know Him thus no longer. Therefore, if anyone is in Christ, he is a new creature; the old things passed away, a behold, new things have come!
>
> 1 Corinthians 5:16–17

Paul never used *soul* to speak of a life surviving death. His interest was in the new life given through and by the risen Christ. For the Christian, this new existence has erased the demarcation line between life and death.

> But someone will say, "How are the dead raised? And with what kind of body do they come?" You fool! That which you sow does not come to life unless it dies; and that which you sow, you do not sow the body which is to be, but a bare grain, perhaps of wheat or of something else. But God gives it a body just as he wished, and to each of the seeds a body of its own. All flesh is not the same flesh, but there is one flesh of men and another flesh of beasts, and another flesh of birds, and another of fish. There are also heavenly bodies and earthly bodies, but the glory of the heavenly is one, and the glory of the earthly is another. . . . So also is the

resurrection of the dead. It is sown a perishable body, it is raise an imperishable body.

1 Corinthians 15:35–42

Paul believes these wonderful things are possible not because we have a soul but by reason of the Holy Spirit's granting new life. The soul is the point of contact where eternal life begins through our relationship with Jesus the Christ.

And what does this promise look like in terms of ectoplasm, skin, muscle, tissue, and bone? What is the nature of the shape this soul is to take in eternity? With what substance did Jesus Christ present himself on Easter morning? We do well to be humble and tentative in our answers. When Paul wrote of a spiritual body, he meant not nonmaterial matter but a person filled with the Holy Spirit. While *soul*—or in Greek, *psyche*—is the root word in 1 Corinthians 15:53–54, it is not obvious what shapes this takes.

> For the perishable must clothe itself with the imperishable, and the mortal with immortality. When the perishable has been clothed with the imperishable, and the mortal with immortality, then the saying that is written will come true: "Death has been swallowed up in victory."

We can be certain that our essence returns in the form and shape we have known it in this present life.

And in Between?

But what happens between the last heartbeat and the first moment of eternity? What should we expect on the other side of the last second of earthly life? Unfortunately, the Christian community has not come to a unanimous opinion since Scripture doesn't offer a systematic answer.

Three possible schools of thought teach very different conclusions. Biblical evidence can be offered for the possibility that at the moment of death we are immediately provided a new spiritual body and are in heaven, in the presence of the Lord. While differing on what exactly happens, another group believes Scripture indicates some sort of intermediate state. Before one enters the presence of God, a final period of development brings final perfection. The last group maintains we drop into "soul sleep" analogous to normal slumber. We awake when the time of the resurrection comes.

Scripture indicates the final resurrection comes in the summation of all history in the return of Christ.

> Now we know that if the earthly tent we live in is destroyed, we have a building from God, an eternal house in heaven, not built by human hands. Meanwhile we groan, longing to be clothed with our heavenly dwelling, because when we are clothed, we will not be found naked. For while we are in this tent, we groan and are burdened, because we do not wish to be unclothed but to be clothed with our heavenly dwelling, so that what is mortal may be swallowed up by life. Now it is God who has made us for this very purpose and has given us the Spirit as a deposit, guaranteeing what is to come.
>
> 2 Corinthians 5:1–5, NIV

These passages suggest the new body won't be granted until that time of final reward. Paul seems to refer to such a possibility as "nakedness." Between the time we leave our old body behind and gain the new one, there must be some form of intermediate existence.

Christians believing in soul repose have a number of passages from Paul indicating the idea of sleep. For example:

> That is why many among you are weak and sick, and a number of you have fallen asleep.
>
> 1 Corinthians 11:30

> After that, he appeared to more than five hundred of the brothers at the same time, most of whom are still living, though some have fallen asleep. Then those also who have fallen asleep in Christ are lost. But Christ has indeed been raised from the dead, the first fruits of those who have fallen asleep.
>
> 1 Corinthians 15:6, 18, 20, NIV

> Brothers, we do not want you to be ignorant about those who fall asleep, or to grieve like the rest of men, who have no hope. We believe that Jesus died and rose again and so we believe that God will bring with Jesus those who have fallen asleep in him.
>
> 1 Thessalonians 4:13–14

Martin Luther merged the idea of an intermediate state with soul sleep. His Reformation attack on the Roman Catholic ideas of purgatory led him to explain the delay between death and the final resurrection as "resting in the arms of Jesus" until history has been fulfilled.

On the other hand, theologians make a strong argument that the ideas of both sleep and nakedness are really meant to be taken more metaphorically than literally. The problem is our understanding any and all attempts to depict what is inexpressible and indescribable. Long ago the church discovered how difficult it is to be dogmatic about the many paradoxes of the faith. We must respect the mystery.

Such mystery is not evoked to stifle discussion but to recognize that human experience has limits. Many analogies will always be incomplete and inadequate because eternal issues never quite mesh with time and history. Try explaining to a child that God does not have a beginning! Nevertheless, we can count on the fact that God has the problem under control.

Beyond the Ravages of Time

Paul recognizes the body may sometimes not be in as good shape as the soul. After all, the nature of physical existence is a continual deterioration of the organism. Paul doesn't intend to set the soul over against the body à la Plato; rather, he describes how the work of the Spirit in the soul is not deterred by illness or difficult circumstances. The body may be perishing, but all remains well with the soul. The inevitable demise of the flesh doesn't impede the work of the soul.

> For I consider that the sufferings of this present time
> are not worthy to be compared with the glory that is to
> be revealed to us. For the anxious longing of the
> creation waits eagerly for the revealing of the sons of
> God . . . even we ourselves groan within ourselves
> waiting eagerly for our adoption as sons, the
> redemption of our body.
>
> Romans 8:18–19, 23

Without evoking the heated prophecy arguments among the premillennialist, amillennialist, and postmillennialist, we can conclude the Scripture is clear that the soul comes forth on the other side of death in a form we knew in everyday life under the conditional clues of our former existence. We will be known as we truly are . . . in Christ!

The soul is not so much saved from death as it is redeemed through death for eternal life with the Holy Trinity, Father, Son, and Holy Spirit.

In the Now

Once again the death camps of the twentieth century unexpectedly offer us a final image, not of death but of what the promise of transformation looks like. Millions of people have been inspired by the story of Corrie ten Boom's journey through Ravensbruck. She and her sister Betsie faced the same indignities and torment that Sophie, Father Kolbe, and Elie Wiesel knew. Betsie did not survive. Corrie remembers:

> She seized me again, led me to the washroom window, and pushed me in ahead of her. In the reeking room stood a nurse. I drew back in alarm, but Mien was behind me.
>
> "This is the sister," Mien said to the nurse.
>
> I turned my head to the side—I would not look at the bodies that lined the far wall. Mien put an arm about my shoulder and drew me across the room till we were standing above the heart-rending row.
>
> "Corrie! Do you see her!"
>
> I raised my eyes to Betsie's face. Lord Jesus—what have You done! Oh Lord, what are You saying! What are You giving me!

For there lay Betsie's face. Her eyes closed as if in sleep, her face full and young. The care lines, the grief lines, the deep hallows of hunger and disease were simply gone. In front of me was the Betsie of Haarlem, happy and at peace. Stronger! Freer! This was the Betsie of heaven, bursting with joy and health. Even her hair was graciously in place as if an angel had ministered to her.[3]

A parable that the present sufferings simply can't be compared to what is ahead. Such was the teaching of Jesus.

Chapter 8

CHRISTIANS DISCOVER THE SOUL

During the first three hundred years of the Christian era, the growing church attempted to clarify and understand the faith that the apostles passed on to their successors before the year A.D. 100. Scripture and tradition arose together in a world filled with mystery religions and mystic and esoteric cults vying for the heart and mind of the age. The era was highly speculative, confused, and rife with immorality and strife—and filled with lost souls. The Christian message was truly a light in a dark night.

The spiritual descendants of Socrates, Aristotle, and Pythagoras were well-entrenched and highly respected teachers of the day. Other long-forgotten proponents of far more bizarre ideas roamed the back streets of Rome, Athens, Jerusalem, and Antioch, offering their unique brands of salvation. Philosophical and intellectual combat was as fierce as the world wars of our time. As the dust of argumentation settled, new names surfaced. Pagan ideas were confronted, challenged, and defeated. Spiritual intellects like Justin Martyr, Irenaeus, Athenagoras, Clement, and Tertullian took the stage. Each of these inspired voices added harmony to the melody line penned by the hands of the apostles. Later generations recognized their insights as the church's greatest theological treasures. The church fathers are still our master guides.

As the twentieth century is preoccupied with questions of psychology, their age was gripped by the meaning of the soul. With one foot planted in the world of the apostles and another in the Greco-Roman empire, these theologians were only a stone's throw from the days of Jesus. After Scripture, we listen more intently to their voices than any others. For them, apostolic succession was not a tradition but a matter of personal relationship. They, indeed, have much to tell us.

The following are excerpts from these early apologists, teachers, preachers, and guardians of the faith called the Ante-Nicene Fathers. These thinkers are the most significant writers before the great Nicene Council convened in A.D. 325. Because the earliest texts are in a foreign prose reflective of classic Greek style, the message is often obscured by the convoluted manner in which they wrote and argued. Therefore, I have translated the ancient texts into a contemporary form analogous to translations like *The Living Bible*. Rather than seeking scholarly precision, the insights of the Ante-Nicene Fathers are offered in speech familiar to our ears. Such was the same reasoning that caused the first writers of the New Testament to use Koine Greek, the language of the street, rather than Classical Greek. No attempt has been made to keep these writings in their exact original order either chronologically or structurally; they have been rearranged to present the subject matter in the clearest light.

We return again to a world deeply immersed in questions about the meaning of the soul. These excerpts are the opinions of those people who walked with the people who walked with Jesus and his twelve.

God Must Be the Starting Point

Arnobius

What makes you think you can figure out who made man and originated the soul? . . . Leave this business to God and let Him know the wheres and whys about what always was or just lately came to be. . . . You best be seeking to know the Supreme God rather than asking foolish questions last, when death frees you of the body, you are faced with a worse death!

Don't be deceived with vain hopes and the teachings of presumptuous pretenders who think they know some secret path to God's eternal house. These fortune-telling vagabonds think their magic charms and secret potions will get them into heaven. . . . No one but Almighty God can preserve the soul.

from *The Seven Books of Arnobius Against the Heathen.*

Philosophers Only Speculate
Tertullian

At the moment of Socrates' death, all of his so-called wisdom really came from assumptions rather than confirmed truth. Who really knows anything about what is true without God? And how can anyone find God without

Christ? Can anybody understand Jesus Christ without the Holy Spirit? Is the Holy Spirit knowable without the mysterious gift of faith? Obviously not! Socrates was inspired by a very different spirit from another place.

Some said Socrates had a demon from his boyhood. Because the teaching of the power of Christ hadn't come yet, there was nothing available to Socrates to ward off the influence of evil. So if the pagans proclaimed Socrates the wisest of all, how much greater is Christian wisdom that sends all the demons running.

From God you may learn about that which you get only from God. Nowhere else can you receive only what God gives. Who is going to reveal what God alone has hidden? It's better to rely on what the heavenly Father reveals to us than to rely on human wisdom simply because someone like Socrates is making bold assumptions.

The trouble with philosophers is they disagree on more than they agree about and when they come up with truth they fail to recognize God as the true source of all knowledge. They pretend to be helped by falsehood or lies supporting their claims. They argue around every side of the question while teaching contrary to our standards of faith. What they don't miss of the truth, they infect with their own poisonous ideas. . . . Only God's inspired standard of truth is of help.

The Christian only needs a few words for a clear understanding of the subject. After all, the Apostles forbade "endless speculations." No final solution can be found by men; only what is learned from God will be the sum and substance of the matter.

Paul saw where this false philosophy would lead when he was in Athens where he had a mouthful of arrogant pseudo-intellectuals. Such teaching is like wine diluted with water.

For example, Plato thinks the soul is unborn and unmade rather than originating in the breath of God. Of course, we know the soul has birth and creation. We know that being born is one thing and being made is another. We are brought forth by God and generated in the same way declaring that the Maker is actually our parent. The speculations of philosophers like Plato cannot stand up next to the authority of inspiration.

Call in Eubulus, Critolaus, Zenocrates or even Plato's companion Aristotle and you will discover that they think the soul is made out of "something." Hipparchus and Heraclitus think it's fire; Hippon and Thales vote for water; Empedocles and Critias teach it's blood; and Epicurus says the soul is made up of atoms. . . . They go on and on.

from *A Treatise on the Soul.*

Lactantius

Plato's arguments about the soul contribute much to discussion but they actually add nothing to truth because he didn't understand anything about the real purpose of God's larger scheme of things. He recognized the truth about the survival of the soul but didn't realize the mystery and place of this idea in God's larger plan. On the other hand, we don't teach by doubtful surmising but because our teachers received divine instruction.

Plato reasoned that anything with perception which moves is immortal; he reasoned that without a beginning to the source of motion, the soul won't have any end to its vitality. Unfortunately, this argument would grant eternal life to the animals which can't even talk. Confronted with this problem, Plato added the argument that humans' souls are all the more immortal because we can learn, think, remember, invent, foresee the future, and have other skills the animals don't possess. Thus, Plato thought the dissolvable part of humans goes to the ground at death, while the unity of the soul is released from this fleshly prison and goes to heaven under its own steam. My description summarizes his ideas.

Pythagoras had the same sentiments as well as his teacher Pherecydes who also influenced Cicero. These are eloquent speakers, as was Dicaearchus, Democritus and certainly Epicurus. But even Tullius, who summarized all of their teaching, finally admitted he had no idea what was really true. He concluded, "Only God knows what is reality." Interesting, isn't it? God really is the very source of *our* truth.

from *The Divine Institutes.*

The Origin of the Soul

Lactantius

As God is unseen, so he made unseen things the five senses can't perceive. God is not to be observed by our frail and inadequate sensory mechanisms. Only through the eyes of the mind can we guess at his illustrious and wonderful works.

Anyone who thinks God doesn't exist isn't even worthy to be called a philosopher because they aren't functioning with any more brains than dumb animals since both act only as if a body is all there is to life. These speculators don't think anything exists they can't see. Such people expect the world to operate by chance not providence.

Because God is incorporeal, invisible, and eternal, we can believe he created the soul the same way. Because God creates the soul after his own nature, it will survive the body even though we can't see it within us.

from *The Divine Institutes.*

Tertullian

One point has already been made in my argument with Hermogenes. The soul is formed by the breath of God and not from matter. God's inspired directive is, "The Lord God breathed on man's face the breath of life and man became a living soul." Nothing more needs to be said.

Recognizing the origin of the soul in the breath of God, we know the soul has a beginning. Unfortunately, Plato thinks the soul is unborn and unmade as he writes in the *Phaedus.* Obviously because the soul has a starting point, it has a birth and creation. Being born is one thing, being made is another. Clearly birth applies only to living entities. . . . The mere opinions of philosophers are pushed aside by inspiration.

from *A Treatise on the Soul.*

The Soul of God

Origen

The soul of God may be understood as the only-begotten Son of God. For as the soul moves and has control over everything in the body, so the only-begotten Son is the very Word and Wisdom of God directing the power of God in this world. The soul of God, Jesus came into our world of affliction, humiliation and tears, entering into our pain. Whenever the Scripture speaks of his suffering, the experience is described with the word *soul*. "Now is my soul troubled; my soul is sorrowful, even unto death; no man takes my soul from me, but I lay it down of myself." Therefore, it appears the soul mediates between the weakness of the flesh and the willingness of the spirit.

from Origen *De Principiis*.

The Nature of the Soul

Tertullian

The soul is born with purity but immediately comes under attack by the Evil One who looks at all souls with envious eyes. From the very portals of birth, the Evil Spirit springs into action to entrap the soul. Idolatry was the midwife assisting at each of our births.

from *A Treatise on the Soul*.

Methodius

O virgins, our souls come into this world with a beauty that is not unlike divine wisdom. The human soul is most like the God who begot and formed us reflecting the image and likeness of the Father, the countenance of an immortal and indestructible shape. The soul's unbegotten beauty is without beginning, not corruptible or changeable, doesn't age or need anything. The Creator encompasses everything with his power and made the soul after his own image. Of course, the result would be unsurpassed beauty.

Therefore, evil spirits love the soul and plot to defile the Godlike image. Their intent is analogous to the condemnation Jeremiah heaped on Jerusalem. "By the roadside you sat waiting for lovers, sat like a nomad in the desert. You have defiled the land with your prostitution and wickedness." The devil and his angels are vile lovers whose intimacies pollute the mind. They try to co-habit with the soul already promised to God.

from *The Banquet of the Ten Virgins*.

Justin Martyr

The soul certainly is alive. What it touches comes to life just as motion moves what it touches. No one would deny the soul lives. But what makes it alive? The answer is simple . . . God.

God wills the soul to live. Life is not its attribute but a characteristic of God, himself. Only the will of God keeps the soul alive and subsequently sustains the body as well.

From *Dialogue with Trypho*.

Irenaeus

The soul isn't life any more than the body is the soul but both partake of the life that comes from God. This is why the Bible says of the first human being, "He became a living soul." Therefore, life and the soul are two different things. The soul goes on living and enduring because of the touch of God imparting perpetual duration.

From Iraenaeus *Against Heresies*.

Soul Capacities
Tertullian

When it comes to knowledge, nature is the teacher and the soul is the pupil. Everything the teacher instructs comes from God, the Teacher of teachers. Look within yourself and you'll get some idea of how much the soul contains. Consider what enables you to think; ponder the abilities of the prophet. Even in a fallen condition, the soul does not forget its Creator. . . . Undoubtedly, the soul existed before the alphabet, speech before books, and ideas before they were put on paper. . . . Obviously, the scriptures are much more ancient than any secular literature. If the knowledge of the soul comes from any written source, it would be from the scripture. . . . What difference does it make whether soul knowledge came from God or from His Book? . . . If you believe in God and Nature, then have faith in the soul. On that basis you will be able to believe in yourself.

from *The Soul's Testimony*.

The Shape of the Soul
Tertullian

The fact internal organs don't detect the existence of the soul doesn't mean anything. Many kinds of non-material entities affect the body. Sound comes into the ear and color into the eyes as smell goes up the nose. You can't hold any of those experiences in your hands either.

Therefore, the lack of specific shape doesn't give rise to any particular conclusion. As the body is nourished by physical substance, the soul is fed by spiritual food such as the study of wisdom.

Chrysippus must have been hallucinating when he claimed two bodies can't be contained in one in order to refute the nature of the soul. Every day, pregnant women give birth to one, two, or even three babies. One Greek woman had four! Even the creation witnesses to how the soul can reside in the body.

We can forget about philosophers' objections. The Gospels offer clear evidence that the soul has a corporeal nature. Luke's story of Lazarus and the rich man in hell are absolute evidence that the soul goes forth in a material form. The torments of hell wouldn't make any sense unless people had a bodily shape. What resides in Hades after departure from the body and waits for the Day of Judgment? Is the soul just a "nothing" in this subterranean world? It certainly is nothing unless it has bodily shape and substance. Punishment and reward require a body. . . . An incorporeal thing has no capacity to suffer or to feel anything.

We don't know of any other shape but a human form. . . . The inner man is different from the outer but they are still one person. The inner must have its own special eyes and ears allowing people like the Apostle Paul to encounter the Lord.

from *A Treatise on the Soul*.

Gregory Thaumaturgis

Thus the next question is, "How is the soul in the body?" Surely the soul cannot be all jumbled up and scattered throughout the body or it would cease to have any significant function. Yet we can't quite say it is a body within the body or it could be weighted. Though the soul is incorporeal, it can't be a body because the soul doesn't have a nose, eyes, ears as a body must. No, the soul is a singular entity while the body is complex made up of many parts.

While the body must be nurtured by food, the soul is fed by reason. Qualities like righteousness, courage, and hope cannot be seen but they are still real. These analogies from virtue help us understand how the soul is different but still has substance. . . .

Most things don't have any power within themselves but depend on an outside force to animate them; when the power stops everything quits. In contrast, the soul is self-activating and never stops. Whatever is self-acting will be ever-acting. Therefore, it follows the soul must be incorruptible and immortal.

from *On the Subject of the Soul.*

Spirit and Soul
Tertullian

Some argue the soul contains a spirit of a different composition from the soul. No, the spirit is in the soul like breath in a person. Their argument is based on the idea that all animals have lungs and windpipes. But it's nonsense to compare the human soul to the workings of a gnat or ant. . . . One can't split soul and spirit apart because they can't be divided. We are on much firmer ground to believe soul and spirit are one.

When we speak of spirit in regard to the soul, we must make careful distinctions. When people teach about breath, spirit, respiration, and certainly the Spirit of God, the terms can become quite confusing. Looking at the question from a human point of view, we must maintain that the soul is breath and not spirit in the distinctively biblical sense of the Spirit.

We could go on quickly if it were not for some heretics with the strange idea that the soul receives a sort of spiritual germ bestowed by mother Sophia (Wisdom) without the Creator's awareness. Scripture saves us from this blind alley by simply saying God alone breathed on the face of humanity and we became living souls.

A clear distinction between spirit and soul is made in such passages as Isaiah 57:16, that I translate, "My Spirit went forth from me, and I made the breath of each and the breath of my Spirit became soul." Again in Isaiah 42:5, I translate the verse, "He gives breath unto the people that are on the earth, and Spirit to them that walk thereon." Therefore, as the result of the work of God's breath, the soul comes first and then afterward the Spirit descends in order to discipline sinful flesh.

The point is that at birth we do not naturally have either the Spirit of God or the devil. The soul stands by itself. We must be concerned about the spirit of the devil entering us. For example, Judas was one of the elect, an apostle, but look what happened when his soul was captured by the Evil One! On the other hand, consider the wonderful thing that happened to King Saul when the Spirit fell on him. He was literally turned into another man and became like one of the prophets! But be warned. Later an evil spirit attached itself to Saul and he turned back the other way and became apostate. You had best take good care of what enters your soul!

from *A Treatise on the Soul.*

Our Difference from Animals
Lactantius

Animals don't have a religion. They have no knowledge of God. Just look at the difference in how animals and people walk. Animals face the ground while we look at the heavens. We alone are both heavenly and earthly having been raised up out of the earth. We know the highest good has to be sought in the loftiest place with God on high. Called by Trismegistus "the contemplation of God," meditation is not impossible for the beasts. We have wisdom which is nothing else but the knowledge of God and this doesn't perish as the animals do.

We also have virtue which is a proof of immortality. With the animals, we share the pleasures of a physical existence. If we seek nothing but pleasure, we will soon die like animals. Virtue teaches us the discipline to endure painful experiences in order to find a higher good. Choosing the better way brings us to immortality.

from *The Divine Institutes.*

A Recap
Tertullian

The soul has freedom of will, control over the animals and other aspects of nature, capacity to foresee the future, and occasionally a true gift of divination. Springing into existence from the breath of God, the immortal soul has shape, form, intelligence, and is self-contained. An archetypal pattern has given to all souls rationality and the ability to develop their capacities through self determination.

from *A Treatise on the Soul.*

Deception, Sin, and the Soul

Tertullian

The supreme powers are the Lord God and his adversary the devil. People tend to think wrongly that fate, necessity, and free choice determine what happens.

The soul is naturally rational. What else would the breath of God produce? Irrationality comes later through the bite of that old intrusive serpent. . . . The devil is the source of our incentive to sin. Because all sin is irrational, this tendency is from the Evil One. Of course, sin and irrationality are completely foreign to God.

Our Lord demonstrated three important qualities of the soul. His teaching was *rational*. The sin of the scribes and Pharisees provoked *indignation* in him. Finally, *desire* was expressed when he said, "I have earnestly desired to eat this passover with you." Everything our Lord thought, envisioned and wanted was ordered with perfect reason. God's anger with the people deserving his wrath will be perfectly logical. He will express indignation against evil people.

from *A Treatise on the Soul.*

Tertullian

When we say there are demons (since we alone cast them out of men's bodies and thereby obviously prove their existence), some disciples of Chrysippus start to pucker up. Yet their attitude only proves the reality and the distasteful nature of the subject. Satan, the angel of evil, is the source of error and contamination in the world luring people into disobedience. . . . He is the destroyer!

from The Soul's Testimony.

Origen

The physician of our souls knows everything necessary for our spiritual health. If through excessive eating and drinking, we cause our own bad health, we expect to take unpleasant and painful medicine. A terrible condition may require amputation. The worst problems have to be burned out of the flesh. How much more will the soul doctor care about the defects caused by sin and crime? Punishment of fire may even be needed for those who have become emotionally and mentally unstable. Scripture warns that God uses similar methods to redeem us. Deuteronomy 28 threatens fevers, colds, and jaundice, as well as other aliments to get our attention. Other passages greatly expand the list of possibilities. The lapsed as well as those who have fallen into everyday forms of sin can expect to drink from God's cup of fury. . . . However, God's vengeance purifies the soul. Remember fire is for healing! Isaiah said, "The Lord will wash away the filth of the sons and daughters of Zion, and shall purge away the blood from the midst of them by the spirit of judgment, and the spirit of burning." . . . The Bible also says, "The Lord will sanctify in a burning fire." Malachi wrote, "The Lord sitting will blow, and purify and will pour forth the cleansed sons of Judah."

from Origin De Principiis.

Lactantius

When we have offended, we must immediately confess, repent and seek pardon from God. Repentance is a great comforter and healer, curing old wounds and offering safe harbor. We must always be ready to be obedient to the Lord. Humility is dear and precious in his sight. If the Lord accepts back both a sinner and a haughty man who confesses, how more will God restore the just person who repents of error. Such a person will be exalted in proportion to their humility! True worship is the offering on the altar of God the pledge of our own minds.

from *The Epitome of the Divine Institutes*.

Lactantius

If people despise virtue and throw themselves away on lusts, they will eventually be smashed into the ground. In contrast, those who seek the highest things of God will not be enslaved to the earth but will gain eternal life.

from *On the Workmanship of God*.

When Death Comes
Tertullian

Death obviously separates the body and the soul. Some philosophers nonsensically claim a soul occasionally stays with a body after death for a period of time. Plato has similar ideas in his *Republic*. There's no point in building theories around the illusion that some people look better for a longer period after death as if the difference is because the soul has lingered. Death conclusive tears everything apart.

133

Even the gentlest death does violence. The companionship of soul and body is like the relationship of two sisters suddenly divided and torn asunder. Even if our last breath is filled with joy, death is still a violent expulsion of the soul from the body. We die at the very moment when we might go on living a life of joy and honor, peace and pleasure. As ships face terrible storms, we must live with the shipwreck of life. What difference does it make if the body dies with broken timbers or is smashed in a storm should we have lost the ability to navigate our soul?

The soul is indivisible because it is immortal. We conclude death is an indivisible process. Death isn't just a natural consequence of being alive but is a result of a fault or defect. Our own arbitrary choice of sin brings death. If the human race didn't sin, death wouldn't follow.

from *A Treatise on the Soul.*

Tertullian

When the animal spirit that drives the body like a charioteer starts to fail because the body is deteriorating, the soul gets ready to depart. If death is rapid because of decapitation, breaking the neck or some such thing, the soul quickly departs. When death is slow and drawn out, the soul also leaves at the same pace.

However, the soul is never fractured or broken into parts by the death process even though the last remnant may seem to be only a diminished portion of itself. The soul doesn't dissolve. The last of the whole is still the whole. In those final moments, the soul almost seems to be able to speak of both worlds, the one being left and the one ahead.

Plato's *Phaedo,* described the body as a prison but the

apostles considered it to be the temple of the Holy Spirit belonging to Christ. Nevertheless, the body still obstructs and obscures the soul. The soul's natural light is diminished similar to our looking through a dirty window. Once the soul is released from the body, it is cleansed and purified. Light pours in. New liberty restores the full potential of the soul like one waking up from a nap and leaving the world of dreams behind. Seeing the very faces of the angels, the soul knows it's home.

from *A Treatise on the Soul.*

Hades: The Land of Beyond[1]
Tertullian

Peter's first letter tells us during the three days Jesus' body was in the tomb, he was actually in the place of the dead ministering to the previously departed. Before he ascended to heaven, Jesus Christ went, like every human being, to this final place so the patriarchs and prophets would be able to receive him. Don't be put off by people who don't want to accept this fact of existence in Hades as if they will go straight to heaven in a manner that makes them better than their master. These believers sound like they would reject their place in the great resurrection if they had to receive it while waiting and resting on the bosom of Abraham.

Therefore, if Christ descended into hell what makes us think we won't wait there? No, we won't ascend up to heaven where he is on the right hand of the Father until we hear the archangel's trumpet blow. Then, with the people on earth, we will together be caught up to meet him in the air. Right now, heaven isn't open to anyone.

When this world passes away then the kingdom of heaven will be open.

Does this mean in the meantime we have to sleep in Hades with the likes of the boy-loving Plato? Arius? Float around the moon with Endymions of the Stoics? No, there is a difference in where the prophets and patriarchs were. Remember that in John's Revelation of a special region in Paradise, he saw exclusively the souls of the martyrs kept together under the great altar. Similarly, the wonderful martyr Perpetua at the time of her death looked into eternity and saw only her fellow-martyrs in Paradise. This place has a special reception room to receive such uncommon newcomers.

Recognize the difference in the death of the pagan and the Christian. If you have to lay down your life in the agony of martyrdom, take up your cross gladly. Your own life's blood is the only sort of key to unlock Paradise. Don't worry! Every soul is kept in safe keeping in Hades until the day of the Lord.

from *A Treatise on the Soul.*

An Intermediate State?
Tertullian

Are there special reasons some souls are detained on earth immediately after death? Is there a temporary removal from Hades during the interim time of waiting?

Some philosophers have said the soul can't depart until the dead are properly buried. Remember Homer's story of Patroclus pleading for Achilles' burial so he could enter Hades? Homer was talking about the rights of the dead in more than poetic imagery. He had the idea that delayed burial injured the soul. However, only vanity could suppose the soul is worried about the rites and rituals for disposing of the body. Why should the soul be concerned about getting rid of the millstone around its own neck? If the soul should be reluctant to face death, wouldn't a tardy arrival in Hades be preferred? No, none of this speculation adds up.

Some of these same people conjecture that a premature death condemns souls to wander across the earth until they have completed their residency requirements for time on the earth. No, either our length of life is appointed by God or not. . . . Really, how could anyone fulfill time requirements on this earth without having a body?

Therefore, regardless of age at the time we die or how death occurs, every soul remains in Hades until the fulfillment of the ages comes at the summons of the angels. We cannot avoid an exile in Hades.

Perhaps, we need to define more carefully what we mean by the word *Hades* because there are two regions in that place, one for good and the other for the bad. Evil people belong there even now. On the other hand, we need not be apprehensive about time spent in a place worthy of the purity of infants and virgins.

Once we're clear that all souls wait in Hades, we can ask about what happens during this detention time. Is there discipline or consolation? Do we just sleep? No, the soul doesn't even sleep during the time we are alive. Only bodies sleep.

In short, "the prison" described as Hades in Matthew 5:28 and the demand to pay "the uttermost farthing" means that even the smallest offense must be recompensed before the time of the resurrection comes. The soul undergoes compensatory discipline during its time in Hades but the refinement of the soul is different from the full accounting demanded at the final resurrection.

from *A Treatise on the Soul.*

Our Hope
Arnobius

We have been taught by the greatest teacher that our souls are always close to the snapping "jaws of death." Yet if we study to know Him, the Supreme Ruler, his kindness will sustain us longer in this world because the knowledge of God is a vital force that cements life together. Otherwise, everything would truly fly apart.

Fear of death and concern for the ruin of our souls is worthwhile because we are prompted to hold fast to him who alone is able to deliver us from eternal danger. Foolish people think their future depends on themselves and they act like they are gods.

We are highly aware of our weaknesses and know we don't have wings to fly upward. Utter dependance on God is our only hope. Christ has promised eternal life. No one can call us foolish for bowing down and worshiping him from whom we will receive these blessings. We expect to receive from Christ escape from a death of suffering and then receive eternal life.

Our detractors argue, "If Christ came to deliver unhappy souls from death and destruction, what about the people who died before he came? What became of these unfortunate people?" . . . You can count on the fact that God's kindness is extended to everyone without favoritism. The trouble with such questions is that there are no complete answers. We need to change our arrogant and conceited attitude, so we can learn what Christ would have already taught us if we had been listening.

Another question is hurled back at us. "If Christ came as the savior of everyone, isn't everyone saved?" I answer, "He frees all alike who ask alike." The fountain of life is open to everyone to drink. If anyone thinks they are so smart that they consider the offering of Christ to be ridiculous and meaningless, why should he go on inviting that person to come to the waters? . . . God neither compels nor terrifies anyone. Our salvation isn't necessary to his well-being but it *sure* is to ours.

from Arnobius *Against the Heathen.*

Chapter 9

THE SOUL
PREVAILS

The first decades of the third century were an
extraordinary time in the history of the church.
After more than one hundred years of persecution and
attack, Christians not only gained respectability and acceptance, the church became the foremost institution in the
declining Roman Empire. By seeking the well-being of
their souls at the expense of their lives, the faithful ended
up also gaining the world!

Supposedly, the Emperor Constantine saw a cross in
the sky. More likely he read the handwriting on the wall
and recognized the wisdom of paying attention to which
way the political tides were flowing. Constantine needed
the Christians much more than they needed him. In A.D. 313,
his Edict of Milan declared an end to all hostilities toward
believers. Immediately church leaders ceased to be sport
for the Colosseum and bait for the lions. Bishops, priests,
and theologians were sought after by the emperor for their

sage advice and godly directives—and ability to keep the ship of state from sinking.

In truth, the badly declining remnant of the once-mighty Roman Empire needed every ounce of political unity that could be mustered. The church appeared to be the strongest and most cohesive group that might hold things together. In order to appropriate the resources of the Christian community, Constantine carved out a new alliance between church and state. It was given to the church to sit at the right hand of the emperor. Even though Jesus instructed Pilate that his kingdom was not of this world, Constantine did everything possible to create a new way of doing business.

By this time, ideological controversy was not new to the church fathers, having for eleven decades battled serious attempts to erode "the faith once delivered." The word *heresy* simply meant doctrine contrary to the apostles' teaching, and there had been plenty of *that!* From the bizarre gnostic ideas of Marcion to the ranting and ravings of the Montantist, no small number of heretical writers had even used the apostles' names as pseudonyms to make their deviant ideas acceptable. The unsettling and disquieting effect of these detours had been a major reason for the compiling of Scripture and the rise of creeds. The traditions, writings, and teachings of the Ante-Nicene fathers were important road signs for the faithful to follow. But controversy had not ended when Constantine waved the white flag.

The emperor's political sensibilities gave him pragmatic concerns about the colliding religious viewpoints in his empire. Unanimity at the altar meant a better chance for unity at the polls. Constantine's influence became an unexpected source of encouragement for further clarification of how the teachings of Jesus and the apostles were to be understood.

In the year A.D. 325, the greatest minds of the Christian community were called by the church and state to assemble at the little town of Nicea to hammer out a statement of faith that would guide the empire and the Christian world even to this very hour. The Nicene Creed was to become the most comprehensive and succinct statement the church would ever develop.

Behind the scenes of the frantic wrangling over words and concepts strange to us (gems such as *ousia, homoousia substantia, persona, essence,* and *being*) was an even more profound concern for the well-being of the soul. Constantine wanted cohesiveness; the church demanded fidelity. Believers' souls dined on truth. Verity was not negotiable, lest the eternal future of the faithful be jeopardized by deadly error.

Questions were raised from many sources about the nature of Jesus' soul. Strange answers were given. Apollinaiarians proclaimed Jesus of Nazareth did not have a human soul. Sabellians erased any line between the Father and the Son while Arians preached Creator and Christ were of completely different substances. The Photinian heresy stripped away all divinity from the Christ and the Manicheans argued to the contrary: There was no humanity in Jesus. Such debates about the nature of the soul were of critical importance to the future of the church. The stakes were even higher than in the previous century.

The work of the Nicene Council was conducted with profound seriousness. These issues were larger than mere ideas, more important than whether Plato would prevail over Aristotle, Athaniasus over Arius. Because the soul fed on God's Word and was nourished by virtue, false teaching could be the equivalent of feeding a baby poison.

The writings of the Ante-Nicene fathers had been like

a great funnel pouring into this council insights and conclusions. After Nicea, the hourglass opened up once again for fresh reflections to flow forth across the Empire, based on the new standards for correct doctrine.

Times were different now and new viewpoints could emerge. Once again, we meet the most profound and spiritual minds the Christian community ever produced. No intellect towers higher than St. Augustine. From the backwaters of the obscure monastery at Hippo, his writings would reshape the world and become the basis for medieval society, prevailing for a thousand years.

We turn now to the Nicene and Post-Nicene fathers, voices continuing to speak of things unseen and the meaning of the soul. After A.D. 325, they carry the questions forward, always seeking paths that will take the faithful on to spiritual maturity. Adapted to modern speech and thought forms, their writings still inspire us even after more than fifteen centuries. They want to help us find our souls.

How Debate Got Started

In St. Augustine's preface to *De Anima Et Ejus Orgine* is an explanation and vignette, a picture of how the debates and writings of the ancient world developed and circulated. His prologue offers helpful insight in understanding how these theological treatise evolved. (And why matters got so hot so quickly.)

St. Augustine

A Vincentius Victor discovered one of my priests, a presbyter named Peter over in Mauritania Caesariensis, one of my little churches, had one of my pamphlets on how the soul originated in the human race. My writings confessed I wasn't sure whether souls came from the first primeval soul of Adam or whether they are assigned to us through, the biological process from whence we come. However, I was quite sure the soul was spirit and not body. Unfortunately that set Vincentius off!

The monk Renatus brought me two of Vincentius books on the soul he had addressed to Peter. I couldn't believe my eyes! This guy was actually attacking *me*. To correct the mistakes in his two books, I had to write four books, one to Renatus, another to Peter, and two more to the poor man himself.

Of course, I had many specific answers to his questions but I had to defend my hesitancy about being dogmatic about the origin of souls. This Vincentius could have been simply denounced, but I tried to be as gentle as I could with the fellow. He wrote back and gave me a rationale for his motivations. Well, draw your own conclusions about my perspective. I addressed the book to Renatus with "Your sincerity impresses me." The salutation I wrote to the priest was, "My dearly beloved brother and fellow presbyter." The books to Vincentius Victor began, "I felt a duty to try and help you."

The Nature of the Soul

The Post-Nicene writers built on the foundations laid by their predecessors, further expanding the general view of what the soul is, does, and becomes in the light of the Nicene Creed. Questions still remained about the origin of the soul. Augustine was the expert.

Origins
St. Augustine

"The human soul is in a unique sense immortal though not absolutely immortal as God alone is. The Scripture points out the soul *can* die. Remember, "Let the dead bury their dead"? Once alienated from the life of God, the soul loses its true life. The soul is not a part of God or it would be truly indestructible and incorruptible. Of course, mere reflection will tell any of us how limited we are.

Philosophers arguing for the soul's participation in God may say sin is the result of the corruption brought on by the body. So what! If the soul sins, it dies. What difference where the problem comes from, the result is the same. The heavenly Father remains holy while the soul becomes tainted. God and the soul are two very different matters.

Remember that the soul is immaterial, not a substance. Whether one defines matter as essence, substance, or some other term it is important for us to know what we are talking about. In order not to be confused, we must be clear that the soul's guidance and direction over the body makes its nature immaterial because the soul can't be located as if it resided in one specific place giving out orders.

For example, the mind is not material in the same sense earth, water, air are material. The soul has its own unique composition superior to anything in this world. This substance cannot be picked up and identified by any of the senses of the body.

I am convinced sin comes to the soul purely by its own free will and choices. It is not God's fault or a mistake in the way we were created. Even though we get into trouble because we want to, we can't free ourselves from sin by will power or self-sacrifice. Only by the grace of God revealed in Jesus Christ can we find salvation. Every single human soul must receive his mediation and sacrament of grace or face the consequences, judgment, and punishment. When we are regenerated in Christ we become a part of his holy fellowship, the church, not only surviving the death of this present body but receiving a new body in glory.

from *Letters of St. Augustine*

St. Augustine

God made humans in his own image. The soul was endowed with reason and intelligence for dominion over the creation. As He formed us from the dust of the earth, God breathed the soul into existence.

from *The City of God*

St. Augustine

What's the soul? Think about the subject and reflect. I don't want the credit for these ideas; I want you to find the truth within yourself.

Did I miss something? Are we only in the image of the Son? Just the Father? Maybe the Holy Spirit? No. Genesis says, "Let us make man after our own image and likeness." The Father does not act without the Son, the Son without the Father, and all in concert with the Holy Spirit. "Our image" means we bear the full image of God.

Sermon II of *Sermons on New-Testament Lessons*

St. Augustine

For heaven's sake don't ever let anyone persuade you that the soul partakes of the nature of God! To believe the soul is part of God is a terrible heresy. The worst heretics say that the soul emanated out of God. We don't even say that the Father, Son, and Holy Spirit are one and the same thing but maintain their separateness. The same is true of the soul, what you must say is that the soul comes from God as a gift, and gift alone.

Teachers contradict themselves when they say the human soul is out of God. The soul would then have the same nature as God. Right? Well, God has no beginning as the soul does! Everything must have no beginning or begin with God's action. Get the point?

Consider the blessed Trinity. Father, Son, and Holy Spirit are one and the same nature and yet separate. The Three together are one God, unchanging, eternal, without beginning or end. However, whatever is created is by definition "creature." All creatures come from *of God* and not made of His nature. He created the world ex-nihilo, out of nothing. We come "out of Him" only in the sense God initiates our existence.

from *On the Soul and Its Origin*

St. Augustine

I must say a final word to people like Vincentius Victor who maintain the soul is not a portion of God but won't admit it is made from nothing. They end up trapped in their own circuitous and faulty logic. God either creates out of nothing or out of Himself. Vincentius actually goes full circle and ends up affirming what he started out denying.

Since the soul was not created out of God Himself, the soul is either breathed by God into being or made out of his breath but in either case the soul comes into being out of nothing. . . . Far be it from me to say the heavenly Father couldn't make the breath of life out of nothing. The point is anything coming directly out of God would be immortal in the same way He is. Of course, the soul is of a different order.

from *On the Soul and Its Origin*

St. Augustine

Remember in the inter-testamental story of the Maccabeans, the mother said, "I cannot tell my sons how you came into my womb?" Obviously, this faithful woman knew she conceived by her husband and that God was the Creator of all life. She was confessing her ignorance of how the human constitution fully operates. She went ahead to say, "For it wasn't me who gave you spirit and soul."

In this same sense, I must say I have no absolute knowledge of how my soul got into my body because I certainly didn't give it to myself. Only the Creator knows whether my soul came through my earthly father by birth or I was given a soul just as Adam got his. I am not ashamed to confess my ignorance of what I can't figure out.

from *On the Soul and Its Origin*

St. Augustine

Right now the soul doesn't have total freedom but is conditioned by the laws of nature. When the heavenly state is attained, the soul will have perfect freedom to govern the new spiritual body. But today we have to live out the cycle of birth, growth, maturity, and death, struggling with the effect of sin on our lives. Even before an infant sins, the little one is still surrounded by the same problem of sinful flesh. Baptism is the best remedy we have for the problem.

from Letters of St. Augustine

Pre-existence

Augustine

And what does Vincentius say of pre-existence of the soul? Something of this order. "The soul attempts to recover its primitive condition which is gradually lost entering life in the flesh because the soul deserved to be polluted by the flesh." Obviously, Vincentius is way over his head and has fallen off a cliff with this crazy idea.

Where does this so-called pollution come from? The soul couldn't have sinned until it got into this world or else the problem started with the nature of God. Now that's blasphemy for sure! Obviously, this man is no teacher!

from The Works of St. Augustine

St. Augustine

The nonsense of Vincentius is that he both maintains the soul was polluted before birth and that the soul had a pre-existence in a blessed and laudable state. Now tell me, how can he both argue for a pre-existence and the soul coming into being out of nothing? He contradicts himself continually. Then he tries to get himself out of this double bind by saying happiness is restored to us at baptism. He has missed the road at every turn. This man should never have suggested any form of pre-existence.

As a good Christian, remember that the apostle said in Romans 9:11, "Children who are not yet born, have done neither good or evil." However could they have any pre-existence when they did nothing?

from *On the Soul and Its Origin*

Resurrection and the Soul

St. Ambrose

Philosophers who speak of the immortality of the soul aren't very satisfying. They only argue for partial redemption. What good is it if the work of God in us fades with time? What do we have if death is the same for the sinner and the just? What good is a miserable immortality?

Paul said, "If in this life only we hope in Christ, we are more miserable than all people." He wrote those words because God has prepared for us another life reserved as reward. We want out of this world to find a new body. Holy men always lamented the length of their lives in this world. David, Jeremiah, Elijah moaned about life in this body.

The soul leaves this world and the problems of the body behind to join with the heavenly company in singing the praises of God. With harps they sing together, "Great and marvelous are your works, O Lord God Almighty, just and true are your ways, King of the nations."

from *On Belief in the Resurrection*

St. Ambrose

If you won't accept the fact of the resurrection by faith, look around you at the examples we see in nature. Grapevines, olives, and many other kinds of fruits are witness to the ongoing cycle of dying and raising again that comes at the end of the year. The resurrection of the dead at the end of all time is equally appropriate. Otherwise, we would sink back into this evil age. For exactly this reason, Jesus Christ suffered on the cross to deliver us from this wicked world. We would be in a heap of hurt if we had to return to life again just to go on sinning.

Many philosophers denied the resurrection of the body but believed in the immortality of the soul. No one by speculation and reason did or could have come to such an amazing truth. Only revelation from God revealed the resurrection of the body.

Book II of *On Disbelief in the Resurrection*

The Struggles of the Soul

St. Chrysostom

We must face the facts about our own sin. Like a not completely tamed horse, we don't like to be saddled with the burden of our guilt; but our reluctance is the work of Satan. We must repent if we are to escape punishment. We can't obtain pardon for our sin if we don't confess. Compassion and kindness await the penitent but we cannot receive pity until after we are ashamed of our deeds.

from *Works of St. Chrysostom, Homily XXI*

John Cassian

Why do we fall into sin? The source of the problem is the corruption of the rational part of the mind and soul where presumptiveness and conceit emerge. Healing of this problem requires humility and a modest perspective on oneself. You will get back on the track when you face the fact of how great your need is. Thinking to be a teacher, you will realize you are still very much in need of a teacher.

We are often tempted and trapped by what seem to be quite reasonable feelings that are nothing more than snares of the enemy. You will remember during the temptation of our Lord in the wilderness, the Evil One attacked the three natural affections of the soul. The natural nature of *desire* was challenged by the temptation to turn stones to bread. The *will to power* was addressed by offering the kingdoms of the world. *Reason* itself was engaged by arguing, "if" you are the Son of God, cast yourself down. Nothing availed because nothing was damaged in the Christ. Take heed!

from *Conference of Abbot Abrham*

St. Augustine

The soul will either be ruled by reason or error. However, error doesn't guide but destroys.

Remember the story of the Samaritan woman at the well? She was ruled by the five senses but error shook her around like a rag doll. Her problem was she wasn't married to the lover she was living with at that moment. In fact, she had gone through five husbands! When she was honest about her condition, Jesus opened her mind. His conversation with her might be understood from a slightly different viewpoint.

"Your problem is your five senses ruled your life," he said. "Now you're beginning to get your mind on a higher plain. But sin in your life and relationships is still distorting your thinking. If you get the iniquity out of your life, then you will even understand who I am."

The woman's perceptiveness was distorted by sin.

from *On the Gospel of John*

St. Chrysostom

I wish I could undress and reveal the souls of those who swear all the time so they could see the wounds and bruises acquired daily because of their foul mouth habit. No one would ever need to say anything to them. The wounds would be more shocking than anything we might suggest.

Since we can't take a peek at the soul, maybe we can look at the rottenness of our thoughts. Remember Ecclesiasticus (Sirach) 23:10 says, "As a servant continually beaten will not be clear of bruises, so the person who swears and names God continually will not be purified in their soul." The mouth that swears all the time cannot but frequently commit perjury. Therefore, I beg you to get rid of this wicked habit.

from *The Works of St. Chrysostam*, Homily XV

Losing Our Souls

St. Augustine

Consider Jesus' meaning when he said, "Let the dead bury their dead." When unbelievers bury a body, both are dead. The one has lost the soul and the others have lost God. For as the soul gives life to the body, God is the life of our soul. Just as the body expires when the soul leaves, the loss of contact with God brings spiritual death. We can't help dying sooner or later, but the death of the soul is by our choice.

Sermon XII of Sermons on New Testament Lessons

St. Ambrose

Pay attention! We face three possible deaths. The first one is spiritual followed by natural demise. Finally, there is a death of eternal punishment.

Adam received death both as penalty and remedy. Of course, the world became a difficult place of sweat and toil. On the other hand, death was also given as a cure for the end of this world's evil. I would suggest you Christians not think of natural death as a penalty but as a remedy. Therefore, there is good in death because it removes us from the battles going on in this world.

from *On the Belief in the Resurrection*

St. Chrysostom

Want to know what a dead soul looks like? Remember the story of the rich man and Lazarus, the poor beggar? Now there's a picture for you! The rich man clearly had a dead soul. He ate, drank, and only lived for pleasure. Even now, the unmerciful and cruel are in the same shape. All the warmth of their love and compassion has gone cold and they are no better than corpses. The problem is no small matter because without these qualities a person is already dead.

from *The Works of St. Chrysostom*, Homily VI

St. Chrysostom

I have a word for people who recognize no boundaries and take advantage of people and also something to say to their victims. Bear their arrogance generously for they are ruining themselves, not us. While they defraud us of our money, the cheats divest themselves of the good will and assistance of God. Though clothed with the wealth of the world, such persons are the poorest of all. True wealth lies in being able to say, "The Lord is my shepherd. I will lack for nothing." Only one thing is required of us. In all things, we are to give thanks to God. On that basis, we have all things in abundance.

from Homilies on Hebrews, Homily XX

The Attack of Evil

John Cassian

No one doubts evil spirits can and do influence what goes on in our thought life. The attacks begin after demons observe our behavior. Our actions, words, and inferences reveal the openings to our soul. Evil spirits can't possibly touch people who protect the inner recesses of the soul.

Greediness is suggested when we already are acting gluttonous. Fornication becomes a thought after the dart of lust is fixed in the soul. Grief, anger, and rage arise first in the heart and then come out in our actions. Just watch what people do and you'll be able to see where the spiritual attacks are going to occur.

from First Conference of Abbot Serenus

John Cassian

We have excellent guidance on the subject of demon attacks on the soul from the blessed Anthony (the Egyptian founder of monasticism). From his own experience of leading a holy life, Abbot Anthony came to understand the attacks of evil very well. He taught that demons cannot find entrance into the mind, body, or soul of anyone until the soul is first deprived of all holy thoughts, emptying it, and distancing the soul from spiritual meditation.

Unclean spirits respond to humans in two ways. Divine grace makes them subject to believers because of our personal holiness. We can demand they not bother us. On the other hand, the sacrifices and gimmicks of the sinful making offerings to evil spirits will lure them on in their attack on these foolish worshipers of evil. Flattered by attention, they will zero in on such people.

The most savage demons would not even venture to approach Anthony when he was making the sign of the cross on his breast and forehead. As he devoted himself to prayer and supplications, the evil spirits returned to where they came from. Christian profession has great power over all fierce and powerful shadows of evil.

from *Cassian's Conference,* chapters 18 and 19

Chapter 10

SPIRITUAL
DISCERNMENT

Long before medieval popes vied with kings for power and influence, the leaders of Christendom were remarkable men and women of extraordinary intellect, spiritual acumen, and overwhelming personal integrity. Gripped by a common quest for a beatific vision of God, preachers, teachers, monks, theologians, martyrs, and laypersons pushed into the interior frontiers of the soul, seeking the sacred space, the Holy of Holies, formerly reserved for entry only by the Aaronic priesthood. No longer concealed from Gentiles by forbidden courts and hanging curtains, the presence of God was open to all who came by the way of the Cross.

Unfortunately, large segments of the Christian community assume the book of Acts is all the story there is to tell. Even those who know something of the history of the Reformation often comprehend little about the likes of Columba, Aidan, Irenaeus, Origen, and the golden-throated preacher John Chrysostom. Blindness robs us of the collected wisdom of the greatest spiritual mountain climbers.

The second, third, and fourth centuries of church history are filled with profound insights into the new life offered in Christ. Behind the intellectual and academic issues raised in those three centuries was a fervent desire to find the way through the barrier separating the world of time and eternity. Convinced that the resurrection of Jesus Christ opened a new path, these early pioneers blazed a trail for the faithful to follow into the spiritual hinterlands.

We turn now to highlights gleaned from their writings. One is quickly aware of having discovered a road map we must travel across our own barren plains and valleys of despair. Tips from these time-tested travelers lift us above the empty preoccupations of our own age and offer us sage insight, clarifying the real from the artificial, the profound from the banal, and the significant from the entertaining. At the end of the trail we will find the hidden treasure of the pearl of great price.

Like mountain climbers gathering around the camp fire in preparation for the next day's ascent to the top of the peaks, we look for the glow of fire and candle reflected in the eyes of these saints who have been to heights of which we have only heard. They know the way home. Let us listen intently to their reflections.

Road Signs and Markers

St. Chrysostom

After an event in the Olympic games, a herald stands up and calls out with a loud voice, "Does anyone accuse the winner? Has there been any cheating?" Character counts in these contests and they aren't nearly as important as what happens to the soul. If such examinations are important in contests revealing the capacity of the body, how much more important is it to inquire about the condition of the soul? We face a similar referee calling out, "Only the holy can draw near."

His call isn't about the forgiveness of sins but personal holiness. The goal is larger than absolution. God wants to know about the presence of the Spirit in our lives and the amount of good works that follow. Not only are we pulled out of the mud, we are meant to be clean and beautiful. Therefore, let us look to the adorning of the soul in golden robes girdled with truth.

from *The Works of Chrysostom*, Homily XVII

St. Chrysostom

Paul tells us to put on the breastplate of faith and love. He is talking about life and doctrine. We must have strong protection to keep anything from piercing the heart. Only faith and love will keep the fiery darts of the devil from penetrating. Where the power of the soul is protected with the armor of love, no secret plot of evil will destroy us. Wickedness, hatred, envy, flattery and hypocrisy cannot infiltrate such a soul. . . . Paul taught that faith, hope, and love abide. He speaks of how important it is to become strong in these particular areas.

from *Homilies on Thessalonians*, Homily IX

St. Chrysostom

Fear of hell won't hurt you any, either. Eccles. 28:6 advises, "Remember your final end." That simple thought alone will help keep you from sin. A soul concerned about the report it must give some day is slow to get into trouble. Fear about the soul keeps worldly tendencies from settling in. Recollecting what *can* happen might be as purifying as any fire.

Unfortunately, fear can sometimes accomplish more than a promise. Many people would forego ten thousand blessings in order to avoid punishment. If people keep hell in front of their eyes, they won't fall into it. On the other hand, those who discount judgment will be the very ones judged. The Ninevites fear of destruction saved them from annihilation. If the people in Noah's time had feared the flood, they wouldn't have drown. Disregarding a genuine threat is a great evil. Nothing is so profitable for the soul as talking about hell.

from Homilies on Thessalonians, Homily II

St. Chrysostom

Discipline is important. Even as we age, it is important to maintain the same disciplines we did during youthful days. Aging causes us to lose the encouragement of youthful vigor.

During our youthful days, we were driven by achievement, desire for status, luxury, lust, and the desire to have everything we see. However, old age depletes the body and cripples our desires. Of course, some old men are intractably stubborn even as they approach death and the final judgment. Of course, this problem is an excess of wickedness. So, don't count on old age alone to cover up the sins of your youth.

from Homilies on Hebrews, Homily VII

St. Chrysostom

Nothing is as contradictory and foreign to the character of the Christian as laziness and being absorbed with this present life. Was your Master crucified to give you a comfortable life? Was Jesus pierced with nails so you could be affluent? . . . Making a pretense of Christianity while living in ease and luxury is contrary to the message of the Cross.

The soul that serves Christ can't avoid a cross. If we are going to live the crucified life, we will love the Cross regardless of the personal cost. Since our Master was hung upon the tree, we must imitate Him. If no one crucifies you, crucify yourself least you bring on a spiritual death! Remember Paul said, "The world has been crucified to me and I to the world" (Galatians 6:14) . . . Baptism is the way of the Cross by which we receive the seal of Christ. Laying on of hands comes through the Cross. . . . Jesus identified suffering as the route of the Cross when he said, "Unless a man take up his cross and follow me, he can't belong to me." We must be prepared to die.

from *Works of St. Chrysostom*, Homily XIII

Storm Warnings

St. Chrysostom

We must learn how to face storms. Notice how boat captains are calm and composed when the tempest is raging while the other people on board are confused and terrified. The pilot sits at the helm calm and undisturbed because he knows the art of sailing. Pay attention and lay hold of the sacred anchor that is our hope in God.

Remember the parable Jesus taught in the Sermon on

the Mount about the house built on the sand? When the tumult came, the edifice crumbled. Unless we are ready for storms, our souls are in danger of being destroyed by less than even a genuine tempest. Simple rumor of trouble may do us in. We will end up being even more foolish than the man who built unwisely.

from *The Works of St. Chrysostom,* Homily XVI

St. Chrysostom

If you say I must live a solitary life to be a good person, you insult virtue. We need to be able to face every difficulty and your soul still prevail. Whether famine or plenty, the Apostle Paul said, "I know how to face abundance and want." Paul gladly took on every difficult circumstance and problem. We should imitate him. We will be the most blessed of people in this life and the next one as well.

Consider a rich man with a wife, children, and every other thing he could want. If he loses all of these gifts and is still virtuous, he is like a rock unmoved by the raging sea. As the captain of a boat laughs during the storm while the children are terrified, so the prepared soul will be tranquil while everyone else is confused. Nothing can disturb the disciplined soul."

from *Homilies on Philippians,* Homily XII

Paths of Righteousness

St. Chrysostom

We must give more attention to making our soul beautiful than using any other adornment we pick up. We have the capacity to decorate a house and wear fashionable clothes.

Apply the same ability to the soul. Remember an ugly bride's defects only become more obvious when paraded around in elaborate dress. In the same way, what is gained if you have expensive carpets in your house while your soul goes about in rags, naked and foul? Take care of yourself, lest like the bride, you make yourself all the more worthless. When people insult us with words, we are appropriately upset yet we don't even notice how we offend our own soul by our misdeeds. Although the hour is late, let us come to our senses and give foremost care to our souls.

from *The Acts of the Apostles*, Homily XXXV

John Cassian

The nature of the soul might be compared to a feather. If it isn't damaged or soaked, a feather naturally sails up to the heaven with the lightness of breath. In the same way, the soul is meant to sail upward to God. We must make sure it is not damaged by physical lusts but carried upward through our spiritual meditations. We do well to remember our Lord's admonition, "Take heed that your hearts are not weighed down by drunkenness and the cares of this world." Therefore, if we want our prayers to not only go up but beyond the sky, we must be careful to purge all earthly faults. Then our prayers will rise unrestrained by the weight of any sin.

from *Cassian's Conferences*

St. Chrysostom

Tell me. If you had a wonderful and admirable husband who loved and treated you very well knowing he would not leave you but would give you anything you desired:

Would you want anything more? Even if you suddenly lost everything but still had such a husband, wouldn't you even think yourself the richer?

So, what are you whining about? Because you don't have a big home? Well, start remembering your sin has been taken away and you have acquired God's good pleasure. Paul said, "We are blessed when we bear everything with thankfulness." Just consider how blessed you will be when, "in all things you will give thanks." If you lose ten thousand pounds of gold, be grateful. By thanking God in all circumstances, you will acquire ten time ten thousand more blessings.

from Homilies on Hebrews, Homily XX

Mountain Climbing

St. Chrysostom

To perfect any art we begin with simple requirements and tender beginnings gradually building up to the more demanding requirements. Like a boy learning to pronounce the letters of the alphabet, we must push on to become proficient at rhetoric. In the same way, we have to begin with simple principles of prayer and mediation. We begin with only a slight idea of what the laws are. We need help in ever keeping the idea of God before our mind. Our minds always tend to wander and slip off into personal reflections and speculations.

from The Works of St. Chrysostom, Homily XXVII

St. Chrysostom

Prayer is a mighty weapon when it's done right. Remember that continued petition has overcome shamelessness, justice, and even savage cruelty. Recall Jesus' teaching about persistence? He told the parable of a friend who beat on the door of the neighbor until the acquaintance got out of bed in the middle of the night. He said, "Because of his importunity the neighbor will rise and give whatever the man seeks to him."

We must apply ourselves to prayer. When offered with sincere earnestness and without self-seeking, powerful things happen. Wars have been stopped and undeserving nations have benefitted. God said, "I have heard their groaning and come down to deliver them." Prayer is like medicine that prevents sin and heals wrong.

We must pray with the humility of the publican crying out, "Be merciful to me a sinner." Then we will obtain everything.

from *The Works of St. Chrysostom*, Homily XXVII

John Cassian

In order to pray like we should, we must observe the rules. First, we must get over being anxious about worldly concerns. Next, we must put out of mind all care and preoccupation with business affairs. In addition, clear your mind of obsessing about other people's defects, shut out chattering noises, silliness, and certainly get rid of anger. A tendency to be depressed must be cleared up. You had better eradicate lust and covetousness by the roots. Cleanse yourself of anything that gets in the way of simplicity and innocence. You will establish a foundation of humility that will support a prayer tower reaching to the heavens.

The soul must be freed of all distracting conversations and roving thoughts that finally drown out our conversations with God. Don't kid yourself. Whatever you were thinking about the hour before you start to pray will return during your prayer. We have to get mentally prepared before we even start the prayer time. Get your mind focused then you can pray without ceasing and feed on continual contemplation of Almighty God.

from *Cassian's Conference*

John Cassian

Another problem we have found in trying to reach the heights through prayer is constant interruption by our colleagues keeping us from remaining in uninterrupted silence. During periods of fasting when we are attempting to get the body under control, the arrival of some brother breaks into the advantage we are seeking through this discipline. Unfortunately, too few people understand the value of the solitary life for prayer.

from *Conference of Abbot Abraham*

St. Chrysostom

Let us stretch our minds toward heaven. Held fast by that desire, we seek to be absorbed and immersed by spiritual fire. Anyone filled with the fire of inspiration has no fear of anyone whether wild beast or man. Armed with fire, this person does not fear traps because he knows danger retreats as he approaches. Such fire cannot be withstood or endured because it is all consuming.

Let us clothe ourselves with heavenly fire that we may offer up glory to our Lord Jesus Christ, with the Father and the Holy Spirit, be glory, might, honor, now and ever, world without end. Amen.

from *Works of St. Chrysostom*, Homily XXXIV

St. Anthanasius

If we choose, we can repent, seek cleaning from our lust, and be cleansed from all defilement of the soul in order to read clearly the Word of God. Even if we are immature and the pressures of life get in the way, the creation itself declares who the Creator is through order and harmony. Divine Scripture teaches us we are made in the image of God. It clearly says, "Let us make man after our Image and likeness." Once the obstacles are removed, the purity of this Image can shine forth and the soul can become like a mirror truly reflecting God. We really can attain to the Image of God himself as his personhood was clearly stamped on Jesus, the Son.

from *Contra Gentes*

Detours and Dead-end Streets

Prior to the first century, the prevailing cultures had absorbed a wide range of strange, esoteric, and mystical religious ideas. The coming of the Christ was a confrontation of what Paul called "the doctrines of demons," evil and intoxicating religious systems feeding on superstition and flourishing in the darkness. As unlikely as it might seem, in our time we have witnessed a return of some of these notions. Although they may come with new names, the substance is the same. Such twisted concepts remain blind alleys.

Both the Ante- and Post-Nicene Fathers spoke to the problem.

Reincarnation

Irenaeus

Our Lord taught not only the continued existence of our souls but that they pass from an earthly body to a renewed body preserving their original form and remembering what happened in this life. Remember the story in Luke 15 of the rich man Dives and the poor man Lazarus in the next life? They clearly recognized each other and remembered the past. Dives wanted to send a warning message back to his relatives from his place of punishment and suffering.

From this story we can conclude: Souls continue to exist, they pass from an earthly to an eternal body, they possess their previous form, memory is retained, Abraham had a prophetic gift, and before the final judgment each person's abode will reflect what they have coming.

from Irenaeus *Against Heresies*

Irenaeus

We can refute the idea of transmigration of souls from body to body (reincarnation) because people don't remember anything about what happened in a previous state. The simple reunion of a soul with the body couldn't possibly extinguish all previous experiences! If transmigration was true, we would have a ton of memories hovering around!

For example, when the body is resting, the soul has no trouble producing dreams and communicating these experiences to the body. If we lived in a previous body for a whole life time, we would have many, many more similar recollections.

from Irenaeus *Against Heresies*

Tertullian

The most damaging philosophers don't care about the soul or the souls of their students when they teach the idea that the soul enters the body at some time after the person is conceived in the womb. We believe the soul is there at the moment of conception. They suggest the soul enters the fetus before complete viability is reached. They say the human seed is deposited ex-concubiter in the womb and then starts to form like bread rising in an oven. Somewhere along the way the soul drops in. The Stoics, Aenesidemus, and at points, Plato himself, teach this heresy. But even the most youngest mother will tell you of the movement of life within us. At the earliest possible moment, she recognizes a real human being is there.

... Even pagan astrologers recognize the soul is present from conception because they made their calculations on the basis of conceptions. Where else would we get our similarities with our parents if not from the seed of the soul?

from *A Treatise on the Soul*

Tertullian

How is a living being conceived?

Remember how John leaped in Elizabeth's womb when Mary came carrying Jesus in her? This response in both women clearly indicated their unborn infants were fully alive. Jeremiah indicated the same when he wrote that God said, "Before I formed you in the womb, I knew you." Was this a dead body Jeremiah spoke of? Certainly not! "God is not the God of the dead but the living."

We maintain that the body and soul are formed at exactly the same time. They are conceived, formed, and maintained perfectly simultaneously. Not a moment of interval exists in their formation. When we die, the separation is simultaneous. Birth is the same.

from *A Treatise on the Soul*

Aronbius

Tell us, Plato, why in the *Meno* do you have a young slave answer questions on mathematics as if to prove what we learn actually comes from the memory of a previous life? Such answers don't come from a former life but from intelligence. Simply following the meaning in your questions leads to insight, not prior instruction. . . . It's much easier to believe we are learning "something" for the first time than it is to accept the idea that the soul is recalling "something" for the first time.

from Aronbius *Against the Heathen*

St. Augustine

What good person could tolerate the idea that a whole lifetime spent in great distress and difficulty fighting off evil and miseries of every kind followed by experiencing the bliss of the contemplation of spiritual life leads to an after life where we lose every achievement of the soul and then return to this life to a start *all over* again? Even worse is the idea we might have to make this return over and over again through endless cycles of going from misery to bliss and back to pain! Such ideas make no sense; especially since the more a person loves God, the more they strive for blessedness. How could we love someone more and more if we thought at the highest moment of relationship, they abandon us? We can't even love human friends if we know they are destined to be our enemies!

from *The City of God*

St. Augustine

Some people think you can't touch anything Plato said. Well, even Porphyry thought amendments were in order. No question that Plato wrote that the souls of men return after death to the bodies of animals. Porphyry got caught up in the crazy logic of this idea. He wouldn't say a mother's soul might return to a donkey that could be required to carry her son. However, he did see the possibility of a mother coming back in the soul of a girl who might end up marrying her own son. Ridiculous!

How much more honorable is our creed and belief coming from angels, prophets, John the Baptist, and the apostles that souls return only to their resurrected bodies.

from *The City of God*

Demons

St. Augustine

Plotinus, who had the reputation of understanding Plato best, says the souls of men are demons. Good men turn into Lares and bad men into larvae. If its not clear whether they were bad or good, they become Manes. Just a glance tells you this idea is like a whirlpool capable of drowning people.

from The City of God

St. Chrysostom

Many simple people think that a violent death turns people into demons. . . . Why did the devil invent such a wicked idea? To undermine the meaning of the death of the martyrs! Of course, the devil couldn't accomplish that goal but he did start another terrible idea. Sorcerers, ministering to the devil, sometimes butcher adolescents hoping to turn them into demons that will return to assist these wicked magicians.

from II Homily on Lazarus

St. Chrysostom

Once the soul is torn from the body, there is no longer any possibility of the soul wandering anymore. The Book of Wisdom says, "The souls of the righteous are in the hands of God." Equally, the souls of the wicked are straight away led to their end. In the story of Lazarus and the rich man, Christ says, "This day they require your soul from you."

from The Works of St. Chrysostom, Homily XXVIII

St. Ambrose

The idea our souls are changed into animals is really wild! How much wilder is the notion that our souls would take the form of a creature so opposed to humanity. Nonsense.

Would the soul spend a lifetime struggling to overcome anger becoming gentle and meek then turn into a roaring lion prowling with unbridled rage seeking bloody slaughter? Let me put it another way. Would a soul's life time pursuit of reason then turn into a wolf's cunning? . . . Obviously, this is an example of how low esteem unbelievers have for each other. Worshippers of animals don't find it strange to think of themselves as turned into animals!

Book II of On Belief in the Resurrection

Pre-existence of the Soul

The seven great Ecumenical Councils of the church defined the final position of the believers on a number of key issues. They took strong exception to some of the ideas expressed by Origen. Even though the great theologian brought light to a number of critical issues, his teaching on preexistence was found wanting. Summation of thought was compiled into a document called *The Anathemas Against Origen*. Nevertheless, the debate leaves behind important information for us in correctly interpreting how the soul is to be understood. The following is a summary of their decisions near the end of this period.

"No one must accept the idea of the preexistence of souls. Anyone who speaks of a created intelligence without a body implying a formless preexistence has given themselves over to the worst of ideas. Even among the other creatures of God, there is definite existence in shape and form with names like cherubim and seraphim, principalities and powers, dominations, thrones, and angels.

If someone claims to have psychic ability because of a pre-existent angelic state and even worse, a demonic existence, they are to be avoided. Some of these people claim they will again return to such a state of existence. The same thing is true for teachers speaking of a twofold race of demons with the souls of people and others with superior spirits ending up as demons. These teachers are of the same camp as those claiming a Nous, a superior intelligence existing before the Blessed Trinity created the world.

We must avoid the idea that the future judgment will be the destruction of the body ending up in existence in an immaterial form of spirit. Such teachers want us to believe the end of all things will be the destruction of matter. They want us to think that we, all the heavenly powers, and the devil will float into absorption into an immaterial amorphous Nous, or great One mind. They are actually saying the Kingdom of Christ will come to an end.

These false teachers also say the soul of Jesus Christ pre-existed with God the Word before the Incarnation and conception of the Virgin. We must declare as anathema the idea that the body of Jesus was formed in the womb of Mary and then later the existing soul came down and was united with the Word of God. In the same manner, we must condemn the idea that in the Great Resurrection our bodies rise in some sort of mystical form different from our present form.

We must avoid strange doctrines as Christ will be crucified again for the demons or that the punishment of demons and evil people will only be temporary. In the same vein, these people teach the power of God is limited."

The Anathemas Against Origen

Chapter 11

THE
RENEWED
QUEST

After the fifth century the civilized world changed abruptly, and radically. The political slide Constantine tried to stop turned into an avalanche. Huns, Visigoths, and Germanic tribes poured into the shrinking Roman Empire, destroying the remnants of a proud past. By A.D. 590, the temporal power of Pope Gregory I was actually greater than the military of the state. Order became chaos, and darkness descended over the world.

The sophisticated writings and arguments of Stoics, Platonists, and Christian apologists were no longer intelligible to the growing number of illiterate peasants, trying to scratch out a living under difficult circumstances. Priests celebrated Latin Masses in a language they could not read or understand. Form was replacing substance.

Across the untamed forests and hinterlands of Europe,

monasteries sprang into existence and candles were lighted again in the dark night. The travels of St. Patrick and his disciples left behind new centers of Christian community. An extremely gifted red-haired young man named Crinthann, or "Fox," began an energetic evangelistic foray across the British Isles and on to Gaul. Generally remembered by the name Columba, the monk returned to Ireland, founding more than forty monasteries. The monastery his successor Aidan founded at Lindisfarne in Northern England was to become the religious wellspring of all English culture.

A new spirituality was emerging. The medieval era would eventually shift its philosophic underpinnings from a Platonic bent to an Aristotelian orientation. In the meantime, the monastic centers spawned men and woman of fervent devotion to prayer, contemplation, and the quest for the beatific vision of God. Leaving the worries, woes, and rewards of secular life behind, monks and nuns gave their undivided attention to the cultivation of the soul.

As the Greeks' inquiries into matter, being, and spirit faded, the new quest was more practical. Seekers were searching for an encounter with God. The now prevailing belief in the resurrection of Jesus and his real presence in Holy Communion spurred the faithful on in their desire for contact with the life of God.

Building on the instruction of Scripture and the insights of the church fathers, the medieval saints left behind a new literature on the soul. Their singular devotion to God still lifts us to the heights and challenges travelers on the rarified atmosphere of the Spirit. We follow these trails into our own time.

Soul Encounters

When in the Fullness of Time
**Hildegard of Bingen, German prophet
and mystic, 1098–1179**

When in the fullness of its time
this creation wilts,
its vigor returns to its own source.

This is the underlying natural law.
When the elements of the world fulfil their function,
they come to ripeness
and their fruit is gathered back to God.

Now these things
are in reference to the soul's life:
spiritual vitality is alive in the soul
in the same way as the marrow of the hips in the
        flesh.

Out of the soul in good standing,
the vigor of the virtues flows out
as do the elements of creation,
it flows back in the same capacity
in attentive prayer.

The soul is a breath of living spirit,
that with excellent sensitivity,
permeates the entire body to give it life.

from *Meditations with Hildegard of Bingen,*
version by Gabriele Uhlein, p. 60.

The Soul Is Oned to God
Dame Julian of Norwich, English mystic, 1343–ca. 1419

The soul,
that noble and joyful life
that is all peace and love,
draws the flesh to give its consent
by grace.
And both shall be Oned
in eternal happiness.
Our soul is Oned to God,
unchangeable goodness,
and therefore
between God and our soul
there is neither wrath nor forgiveness
because

there is no between.

Because of the beautiful oneing
that was made by God
between the body and the soul

it must be
that we will be restored
from double death.

from *Meditations with Julian of Norwich*,
version by Brendan Doyle, p. 31.

The Interior Castle
Saint Teresa of Avila, Spanish Carmelite nun, 1515–1582

*I began to think of the soul as if it were a castle made of a
single diamond or of very clear crystal, in which there are many
rooms, just as in Heaven there are many mansions.*

While I was beseeching Our Lord today that He would speak through me, since I could find nothing to say and had no idea how to begin to carry out the obligation laid upon me by obedience a thought occurred to me which I will now set down, in order to have some foundation on which to build. I began to think of the soul as if it were a castle made of a single diamond or of very clear crystal, in which there are many rooms, just as in heaven there are many mansions. Now if we think carefully over this, sisters, the soul of the righteous man is nothing but a paradise, in which, as God tells, He takes His delight. For what do you think a room will be like which is the delight of a King so mighty, so wise, so pure and so full of all that is good? I can find nothing with which to compare the great beauty of a soul and its great capacity. In fact, however acute our intellects may be, they will no more be able to attain to a comprehension of this than to an understanding of God; for, as He Himself says, He created us in His image and likeness. Now if this is so—and it is—there is no point in our fatiguing ourselves by attempting to comprehend the beauty of this castle; for, though it is His creature, and there is therefore as much difference between it and God as between creature and Creator, the very fact that His Majesty says it is made in His image means that we can hardly form any conception of the soul's great dignity and beauty.

It is no small pity, and should cause us no little shame, that, through our own fault, we do not understand ourselves, or know who we are. Would it not be a sign of great ignorance, my daughters, if a person were asked who he was, and could not say, and had no idea who his father of his mother was, or from what country he came? Though that is great stupidity, our own is incomparably greater if we make no attempt to discover what we are, and only know that we are living in these bodies, and have a vague idea, because we have heard it and because our Faith tells us so, that we possess souls. As to what good qualities there may be in our souls, or Who dwells within them, or how precious they are—those are things which we seldom consider and so we trouble little about carefully preserving the soul's beauty. All our interest is centered in the rough setting of the diamond and in the outer wall of the castle— that is to say, in these bodies of ours.

from *The Interior Castle*,
translated and edited by E. Allison Peers, pp. 28–29.

The Lover of My Soul

The Divine Love of the Soul
**Meister Eckhart, German theologian
and mystic, 1260–ca. 1329**

God
loves the soul so deeply
that were anyone to take away from God
the divine love of the soul,
that person would kill God.

If you were to let a horse
    run about in a green meadow,
the horse would want to pour forth its whole strength
    in leaping about the meadow,

So too
it is a joy to God
      to have poured out

the divine nature and being
    completely into us

who are divine images.

from Meditations with Meister Eckhart,
version by Matthew Fox, p. 29.

The Rapture of Divine Love
Evelyn Underhill, English poet, novelist,
and mystic, 1875–1941

The anonymous author of the "Mirror" writes, in one of his most daring passages, " 'I am God,' says Love, 'for Love is God, and God is Love. And this soul is God by condition of love: but I am God by Nature Divine. And this [state] is hers by righteousness of love, so that this precious beloved of me, is learned, and led of Me without her [working]. . . . This [soul] is the eagle that flies high, so right high and yet more high than doth any other bird; for she is feathered with fine love.' . . ."

I think no one can deny that the comparison of the bond between soul and the Absolute to "ghostly glue," though crude, is wholly innocent. Its appearance in ["The Epistle of Prayer"] as an alternative to the symbol of wedlock may well check the uncritical enthusiasm of those who condemn at sight all "sexual" imagery. That has seemed to the mystics appropriate and exact is proved by its reappearance in the next century in the work of a greater contemplative. "Thou givest me," says Peterson, "Thy whole Self to be mine whole and undivided, if at least I shall be Thine whole and undivided. And when I shall be thus all Thine, even as from everlasting Thou hast loved Thyself, so from everlasting Thou has loved me: for this means nothing more than that Thou enjoy Thee in myself and myself in Thee. And when in Thee I shall love myself, nothing else but Thee do I love, because *Thou art in me and I in Thee, glued together as one and the selfsame thing,* which henceforth and forever cannot be divided."

From this kind of language to that of the Spiritual Marriage, as understood by the pure minds of the mystics, is but a step. They mean by it no rapturous satisfactions, one dubious spiritualizing of earthly ecstasies, but a life-long bond "that shall never be lost or broken," a close personal union of will and of heart between the free self and that "Fairest in Beauty" Whom it has known in the act of contemplation.

The Mystic Way has been a progress, a growth, in love: a deliberate fostering of the inward tendency of the soul towards its source, an eradication of its disorderly tendencies to "temporal goods." But the only proper end of love is union: "a perfect uniting and coupling together of the lover and the loved into one." It is "a unifying principle," the philosophers say: life's mightiest agent upon every plane. Moreover, just as earthly marriage is understood by the moral sense less as a satisfaction of personal desire, that as a part of the great process of life—the fusion of two selves for new purposes—so such spiritual marriage brings with it duties and obligations. With the attainment of a new order, the new infusion of vitality, comes a new responsibility, the call to effort and endurance on a new and mighty scale. It is not an act but a state. Fresh life is imparted, by which our lives are made complete: New creative powers are conferred. The self, lifted to the divine order, is to be an agent of the divine fecundity: an energizing center, a parent of transcendental life.

from *Mysticism,* pp. 427–28.

Sin and the Soul

The Dialogue
Catherine of Siena

Because these three powers (memory, understanding, and will) are dead, everything they do in intention or in fact is dead so far as grace is concerned. They can no longer defend themselves against their enemies. They are helpless unless I help them. But they do still have their freedom of choice as long as they are in the flesh, and any time these dead will ask for my help they can have it—but that is the limit of what they can do for themselves.

They become unbearable to themselves. They who wanted to rule the world find themselves ruled by nothingness, that is, by sin—for sin is the opposite of being, and they have become servants and slaves of sin.

I made them trees of love through the life of grace, which they received in holy baptism. But they have become trees of death, because they are dead. . . .

Now you have seen how deluded these souls are, and how painfully they make their way to hell—like martyrs of the devil! You have seen what it is that blinds them: the cloud of selfish love plastered over the pupil that is the light of faith. And you have seen how the troubles of the world, whatever their source, may hurt my servants physically (for the world hounds them), but not spiritually, because they have identified their wills with mine, and so they are happy to endure pain for me. But the world's servants are hounded within and without—but especially within. They are afraid of losing what they have. And love hounds them with longing for what they cannot have. And words could never describe all the other troubles that follow on the heels of these two principal ones. So you see that even in this life the lot of the just is better than that of sinners. Now you have seen quite fully both the journeying end and the end of the latter. . . .

You know (for I have told you) that some deluded souls clothe themselves in selfish love of themselves rather that walk in the light. They love and possess creatures apart from me, and so they pass through this life tormented, becoming insupportable even to themselves. If these souls do not rouse themselves, they will end in eternal damnation. . . .

I have told you that the will alone is the source of suffering. And because my servants are stripped of their own will and clothed in mine, they feel no grief in suffering but feel me in their souls and are satisfied. Without me they could never be satisfied even if they possessed the whole world. For created things are less than the human person. They were made for you, not you for them, and so they can never satisfy you. Only I can satisfy you. These wretched souls, then, caught in such blindness, are forever toiling but never satisfied. They long for what they cannot have because they will not ask it of me though I could satisfy them.

from *Catherine of Siena,*
translated by Suzanne Noffke

Soul Struggle

Dark Night of the Soul
**Saint John of the Cross, Spanish mystic
and poet, 1542–1591**

On a dark secret night,
starving for love and deep in flame,

O happy lucky flight!
unseen I slipped away,
my house at last was calm and safe,
Blackly free from light,
disguised and down a secret way,
O happy lucky flight!
in darkness I escaped,
my house at last was calm and safe.

On that happy night—in
secret; no one saw me through the dark—
and I saw nothing then,
no other light to mark
the way but fire pounding my heart.

That flaming guided me
more firmly than the noonday sun,
and waiting there was he
I knew so well—who shone
where nobody appeared to come.

O night, my guide!
O night more friendly than the dawn!
O tender night that tied
lover and the loved one,
loved one in the lover fused as one!

On my flowering breasts
which I had saved for him alone,
he slept and I caressed
and fondled him with love,
and cedars fanned the air above.

Wind from the castle wall
while my fingers played in his hair:
its hands serenely fell

wounding my neck, and there
my senses vanished in the air.
I lay. Forgot my being,
and on my love I leaned my face.
All ceased. I left my being,
leaving my cares to fade
among the lilies far away.

The Dialogue
Catherine of Siena

Do you not know, my daughter, that all the sufferings
the soul bears or can bear in this life are not enough to
punish one smallest sin? For an offense against me, infinite
Good, demands infinite satisfaction. So I want you to
know that not all sufferings given in this life are given for
punishment, but rather for correction, to chastise the child
who offends. However, it is true that a soul's desire, that
is, true contrition and sorrow for sin, can make satisfaction.
True contrition satisfies for sin and its penalty not by virtue
of any finite suffering you may bear, but by virtue of your
infinite desire. For God, who is infinite, would have infinite
love and infinite sorrow. . . .

Let every soul rejoice who suffers many troubles, because such is the road that leads to this delightfully glorious
state. I have told you before that you reach perfection
through knowledge and contempt of yourself and knowledge of my goodness. And at no time does the soul know
herself so well, if I am within her, as when she is most
beleaguered. Why? I will tell you. She knows herself well

when she finds herself besieged and can neither free herself nor resist being captured. Yes, she can resist with her will to the point of not giving her consent, but that is all. *Then* she can come to know that [of herself] she is nothing. For if she were anything at all of herself, she would be able to get rid of what she did not want. So in this way she is humbled in true self-knowledge, and in the light of holy faith she runs to me, God eternal. For by my kindness she was able to maintain her good and holy will steadfast when she was sorely besieged, so that she did not imitate the wretched things that were vexing her.

You have good reason, then, to take comfort in the teaching of the gentle loving Word, my only-begotten Son, in times of great trouble, suffering, and adversity, and when you are tempted by people or the devil. For these things strengthen your virtue and bring you to great perfection. . . .

I have told you about perfect and imperfect tears, and how they all come from the heart. Whatever their reason, they all come from this same vessel, and so all of them can be called "heartfelt tears." The only difference lies in whether the love is ordered well or ill, is perfect or imperfect.

I still have to tell you, if I would fully answer your desire, about some souls who want the perfection of tears though it seems they cannot have it. Is there another way than physical tears? Yes. There is a weeping of fire, of true holy longing, and it consumes in love. Such a soul would like to dissolve her very life in weeping in self-contempt and for the salvation of souls, but she seems unable to do it.

from *Catherine of Siena,*
translated by Suzanne Noffke

Christ Speaks to the Faithful Struggler
Thomas à Kempis

"I will hear what God the Lord will speak" (Ps. 85:8). Blessed is the soul which hears the Lord speaking within, and from His mouth receives the word of consolation. Blessed are the ears that catch the pulses of the divine whisper (Matt. 13:16, 17), and give no heed to the whisperings of this world. Blessed indeed are those ears which listen not after the voice which is sounding without, but for the truth teaching inwardly. Blessed are the eyes that are shut to outward things, but intent on things inward. Blessed are they that enter far into things within, and endeavor to prepare themselves more and more by daily exercises, for the receiving of heavenly secrets. Blessed are they who are glad to have time to spare for God, and who shake off all worldly hindrances.

Consider these things, O my soul, and shut up the door of your sensual desires, that you may hear what the Lord your God speaks in you (Ps. 85:8).

Thus says your Beloved, "I am thy salvation," your Peace, and your Life: keep yourself with Me, and you shall find peace. Let go all transitory things, and seek the things eternal. What are all transitory objects but seductive things? And what can all creatures avail, if you are forsaken by the Creator?

Renounce therefore all things, and labor to please your Creator, and to be faithful unto Him, that you may be able to attain unto true blessedness.

from *The Imitation of Christ,*
translated by E. M. Blaiklock

The Soul's Capacities

The Dialogue
Catherine of Siena

Each of you has your own vineyard, your soul, in which your free will is the appointed worker during this life. Once the time of your life has passed, your will can work neither for good nor for evil; but while you live it can till the vineyard of your soul where I have placed it. This tiller of your soul has been given such power that neither the devil nor any other creature can steal it without the will's consent, for in holy baptism the will was armed with a knife that is love of virtue and hatred of sin. This love and hated are to be found in the blood. For my only-begotten Son gave his blood for you in death out of love for you and hatred for sin, and through that blood you receive life in holy baptism. . . .

There are, then, two aspects to yourself: sensuality and reason. Sensuality is a servant, and it has been appointed to serve the soul, so that your body may be your instrument for proving and exercising virtue. The soul is free, liberated from sin in my Son's blood, and she cannot be dominated unless she consents to it with her will, which is bound up with free choice. Free choice is one with the will, and agrees with it. It is set between sensuality and reason and can turn to whichever one it will. . . .

The memory holds on to my blessings and my goodness to the soul. Understanding contemplates the unspeakable love I have shown you though the mediation of my only-begotten Son, whom I have set before your mind's eye for you to contemplate in him the fire of my charity.

The will, finally, is joined with them to know and desire me, your final goal.

When these three powers of the soul are gathered together, I am in their midst by grace. And as soon as you are filled with my love and love of your neighbor, you will find yourself in the company of the multitude of solid virtues. Then the soul's appetite is ready to be thirsty—thirsty for virtue and my honor and the salvation of souls. Every other thirst is now exhausted and dead, and you travel securely, without any slavish fear. You have climbed the first step, that of desire. Once desire is stripped of selfish love, you rise above yourself and above passing things. What you decide to keep, you love and hold not apart from me but with me, that is, with true holy fear and love of virtue.

from *Catherine of Siena,*
translated by Suzanne Noffke

The Quest for the Soul

The Pilgrim Soul
Anonymous nineteenth-century Russian Christian monk
I said, "But I beg you to give me some spiritual teaching. How can I save my soul?"

For a long time I wandered through many places. I read my Bible always, and everywhere I asked whether there was not in the neighborhood a spiritual teacher, a devout and experienced guide, to be found. One day I was told that in a certain village a gentleman had long been living and seeking the salvation of his soul. He had a chapel in his house. He never left his estate, and he spent his time in prayer and reading devotional books. Hearing this, I ran rather than walked to the village named. I got there and found him.

"What do you want of me?" he asked.

"I have heard that you are a devout and clever person," said I.

"In God's name please explain to me the meaning of the Apostle's words, 'Pray without ceasing.' How is it possible to pray without ceasing? I want to know so much, but I cannot understand it all."

He was silent for a while and looked at me closely. Then he said, "Ceaseless interior prayer is a continual yearning of the human spirit toward God. To succeed in this consoling exercise we must pray more often to God to teach us to pray without ceasing. Pray more, and pray more fervently. It is prayer itself which will reveal to you how it can be achieved unceasingly; but it will take some time."

So saying, he had food brought to me, gave me money for my journey, and let me go.

He did not explain the matter.

from *The Way of a Pilgrim*,
translated by R. M. French, p. 4.

The Sleeping Soul
Albert Schweitzer, Alsatian theologian, musician, medical missionary, 1875–1965

You know of the disease in Central Africa called sleeping sickness. . . . There also exists a sleeping sickness of the soul. Its most dangerous aspect is that one is unaware of its coming. That is why you have to be careful. As soon as you notice the slightest sign of indifference, the moment you become aware of the loss of a certain seriousness, of longing, of enthusiasm and zest, take it as a warning. You should realize that your soul suffers if you live superficially. People need times in which to concentrate, when they can search for their innermost selves. It is tragic that most men have not achieved this feeling of self-awareness. And finally, when they hear the inner voice they do not want to listen anymore. They carry on as before so as not to be constantly reminded of what they have lost. But as for you, resolve to keep a quiet time both in your homes and here within these peaceful walls when the bells ring on Sundays. Then your souls can speak to you without being drowned out by the hustle and bustle of everyday life.

from *The Search for Meaning,*
by Phillip L. Berman, epigraph.

The Appearance and Disappearance of the Soul
Jacob Needelman, American philosopher

A hundred, a thousand times a day, perhaps, "The soul is aborted." An individual is completely unaware of this loss and remains so throughout his whole life. Without the necessary help and guidance, he never reaches the orientation necessary for enabling these everyday experiences to accumulate. . . .

"Lost Christianity" is the lost or forgotten power of man to extract the pure energy of the soul from the experiences that make up his life. This possibility is distinct only in the most vivid or painful moments of our ordinary lives, but it can be discovered in all experiences if one knows how to seek it. Certain powerful experiences—such as the encounter with death or deep disappointment—are accompanied by the sensation of *presence;* an attention appears that is simultaneously open to higher, freer mind ("Spirit") and to all the perceptions, sensations, and emotions that constitute our ordinary self. One feels both separate and engaged in a new and entirely extraordinary way. One experiences "I Am." This is the soul (in inception).

It was a disaster for Christianity, according to Father Sylvan, when it adopted the notion that the soul of man already exists in finished form within human nature. This assumption about the given existence of the soul led to our identification of ordinary kinds of thoughts, emotions and sensations with the soul, the higher part of ourselves, and hence to the futile and mistaken effort to perfect our being by perfecting our thoughts, emotions, or sensations, that is, the futile effort of thought to alter emotion or vice versa. The Christian teaching, as Father Sylvan presents it, says on contrary that these psychological functions are incapable of altering each other. Change, transformation, can come only through the action of an objectively higher force: the Spirit. And this Spirit cannot find channels of action unless there exists something in man that can receive it and pass it on to all the parts of himself.

The immensity and revolutionary nature of this idea can be seen when it is applied to the efforts of mankind, everywhere, to find "happiness." The quest for happiness, which in one form or another is the main impetus of the whole mass of human life and moral idealism, is from this point of view little more than the vain effort by the mind to alter the emotions, or vice versa.

But the power to alter the structure of human life, inwardly as well as outwardly, does not reside in a partial function of the psyche. Only that function which can be in actual relationship, actual contact, with all the parts of the self has the possibility of altering the self, or of serving as the channel for the possibility of altering the self, or of serving as the channel for the force that can alter the whole of the self. That function Father Sylvan identifies as the power of gathered attention, the power of the soul.

from *Lost Christianity*, pp. 175–76.

Soul: Possession of
Fulton J. Sheen

The possession of a soul means the undisturbed mastery of oneself which is the secret of inner peace, as distinguished from a thousand agitations which make it fearful, unhappy, and disappointed. Only when the soul is possessed can anything else be enjoyed.

from *Life of Christ*

Soul: Injury
Fulton J. Sheen

But the power to do harm would never affect the souls of the apostles. The body can be injured without the consent of the soul, but the soul cannot be injured without its own consent. The only thing to be feared is losing, not human life, but the Divine life which is God.

from *Life of Christ*

Soul: Fearing Those Who Can Kill
Fulton J. Sheen

When He said: "I have conquered the world," He did not mean His followers would be immune from woes, pain, sorrow, and crucifixion. He gave no peace which promised a banishment from strife; for God hates peace in those destined for war. If the Heavenly Father did not spare His Son, He, the Heavenly Son, would not spare His Disciples. What the Resurrection offered was not immunity from evil in the physical world, but immunity from sin in the soul.

from *Life of Christ*

PART THREE

Recovery:
Where Is the Soul?

Chapter 12

FINDING THE SOUL: AN EXERCISE

We have read the Scripture, studied the church fathers, and listened to the saints. Their experiences offer to us extraordinary insight and encouragement. Now it's time to settle into our own hermitages and move from knowing about to *knowing*. All the material in countless books will do little good unless we put insight into practice. We must now make the solitary journey with no other companion than the resurrected Christ who beckons us to follow Him.

In my soul travels, I found particular road signs and special paths were significant. I offer these discoveries to you as pump primers.

Do Not Fear the Silence

A distraught, depressed pastor once came to the psychiatrist Carl Jung for counsel. Jung asked about the man's work schedule. He proudly reported a consistent sixty-hour-a-week average. Jung's prescription was for the man to go home at 5:00 P.M. each day and spend the next three hours in complete solitude doing absolutely nothing.

The pastor returned in a week with a report of significant relief. He reported happily, "I've been able to read a number of books I had missed."

Jung retorted, "I told you to do *nothing*."

The minister was shocked and explained he couldn't possibly do nothing but be alone with himself for such a long time.

With a wry smile Jung answered, "And you visit *that* on people sixty hours a week?"

Are we really any different? We hit the house and the stereo goes on, the TV is added, and we hope for a phone call. Like the pastor, we fear the shape of absolute silence.

Remember this: no silence, no soul.

In Henri Nouwen's *The Way of the Heart,* his discussion of the desert spirituality of the church fathers warns us about the difficulty of silence today.

One of our main problems is that in this chatty society, silence has become a fearful thing. For most people, silence creates itchiness and nervousness. Many experience silence not as full and rich, but as empty and hollow. For them silence is like a gaping abyss which can swallow them up. As soon as the minister says during a worship service, "Let us be silent for a few moments," people tend to become restless and preoccupied with only one thought: "When will this be over?" Imposed silence often creates hostility and resentment. Many ministers who have experimented with silence in their services have soon found out that silence can be more demonic than divine and have quickly picked up the signals that were saying: "Please keep talking."[1]

No, the task is not easy.

After repeated attempts to get quiet, I began to discover I had a placid place at the center of my being. Before I found the tranquil terrain of the soul, my prayers were words I flung toward the ceiling, desperately hoping something got beyond the roof. After I located this space, I knew I had located the point of connection. Frantic pleading words were no longer necessary. The Spirit began to intercede with groanings and longings for which there were no words.

I suggest you start by setting aside thirty minutes when you will do nothing but wait in silence. If nothing else, you will find this is a marvelous help in remembering everything you should have done earlier. Thoughts and hints of activities will float from all directions. No problem. This interference is par for the course.

I quickly found placing a pad and pencil on the desk was vital. As each reminder came up, I simply wrote the task down and dismissed it from my mind. I didn't have to worry about forgetting, and my mind could be at ease. Like a glass of muddy water settling, distractions drifted to the bottom and clarity returned. Several sessions were required before I got the hang of getting completely quiet.

The goal is not to perform a technique of meditation but rather to get ready to enter the presence of God. The Bible says we are to love the Lord our God with our whole heart, mind, and soul. I found that most of the time I approached God with a willing heart, half a mind, and no soul. The exercise in quietness remedies the problem. The task was to get all barriers of distraction out of the way.

Perhaps a different perspective on silence will encourage you. Metropolitan Anthony Bloom writes:

We have to learn to distinguish two sorts of silence. God's silence and our own inner silence. First the silence of God, often harder to bear than his refusal . . . Second, the silence of man, deeper than speech, in closer communion with God than any words. God's silence to our prayer can last only a short time or it may seem to go on for ever. Christ was silent to the prayers of the Canaanite woman and this led her to gather up all her faith and hope and human love to offer to God so that he might extend the conditions of the kingdom beyond the chosen people. The silence of Christ provoked her to respond, to grow to her capacity. And God may do the same to us with shorter or longer silences to summon our strength and faithfulness and lead us to deeper relationship with him than would have been possible had it been easy.[2]

Only after you become comfortable with the silence are you prepared to go on. If you are seriously reading this book and chapter as a guide to finding the soul, I would suggest you stop at this point and read no further until you have been able to stay in the silence for thirty minutes. More knowledge won't help. Only experience will profit.

Meeting Jesus

Once we are settled in the silence, the task is to meet Jesus, the resurrected Lord. The quest is not a learning experience as much as an encounter with God. The objective is to rejuvenate the soul so we will be able to recognize the real thing as it happens.

Reflections on the Jesus Prayer, by a nameless priest of the Byzantine Church tells us:

> God is present *within* us; He manifest Himself in *our*
> Self and this inner manifestation of God is
> all-important; there is no religious life, no life of the
> Spirit without this; our sanctification and our salvation
> hinge on this. Moreover, this manifestation of God in
> us depends on ourselves; it takes place only if we want
> it to take place.[3]

During my sojourn in the Benedictine monastery, I learned the value of the Jesus prayer. For two thousand years, Christians have dwelt in the presence of their Lord by simply praying over and over the name *Jesus*.

We are not experimenting with some form of mediation or looking for mystical moments. In contrast, we are simply doing what lovers do when they gaze into each other's eyes and find no other words adequate except the other's name. The goal is not petition or intercession but simply affirmation in love.

Often the Jesus prayer is expanded into a longer form. We repeat the prayer of the blind man on the road to Jericho, "Lord Jesus Christ, son of God have mercy on me a sinner." Each word is repeated slowly as we ponder the message while praying the meaning. For example:

"Lord: Jesus you are the Lord of my Life. Thank you for remembering me."

"Jesus: You are God's gift to us. You died for me."

"Christ: You are my Messiah, the One who will lead me to all fulfillment."

"Son: You were truly a human being. You know what my life is about."

"Of God: You take me to the Father. You are the Way, the Truth, the Life."

"Have mercy, forgive my sin: Please overlook my inadequacy.

"On me: Rejoice that I am important to you."

"A sinner: My life would be completely empty, guilty, and without hope without your love."

The Byzantine priest reminds us:

The Jesus Prayer does not end with the word "sinner" for the simple reason that the Jesus prayer does not end at all. "Sinner" is the last word of our exhalation. It empties our lungs. And as we begin to fill them again with out next breath, the heartbeat, starting with the "Lord," begins to beat out the Good News once more. As in a musical rhythm, the last weak beat in the measure serves as the springboard to the strong first beat of the next measure. "Sinner" is the weak beat that leads us to "Lord," and the Lord is our strong beat. And so the dance goes on.[4]

I found that as I prayed and considered each aspect of this prayer over and over again, the sense of presence grew. Equally important for the journey, I began to have a growing awareness of my soul, the God capacity within me. Something long neglected and overlooked was again taking form. Like a weightlifter building atrophied muscles, new form and shape began to emerge.

What is happening during these moments of inner dialogue? The priest of the Byzantine church tells us:

> The eternal Word of God took a body of the Blessed Virgin, died and rose gloriously on the Third Day in that same divinized body. And, because by baptism I became one with that body, and because by Holy Communion I am constantly sustaining that bodily oneness with Christ and growing in it—for these reasons, when I bring my mind down into my heart and listen, I discern not just my own heart-beat, but Christ's. It is because my body is Christ's body that I am a Temple. And my heart (His heart) is the innermost sanctuary of that Temple. Therefore, when my mind is in my heart—and not only my mind, but my animal and vegative drives and energies, too—then I am truly at prayer. For prayer is nothing else than attentiveness to God's presence. God is with us. "Let us be attentive," as we say in the Divine Liturgy.[5]

In this sense, we are not praying as much as learning to pray, because only the Holy Spirit can really teach us how to commune with God. At each step forward into the soul, the hand of Jesus meets us and takes us forward. We think we are doing the work only to discover the divine source of instruction stands behind and prior to any effort on our part. We do not discover the soul as much as we have the soul revealed to us.

The unknown author of the spiritual classic *The Cloud of Unknowing* put it this way, "He kindled your desire for himself, and bound you to him by the chain of such longing."[6] Thomas Merton said it differently: "true contemplation is not a psychological trick but a theological grace. It can come to us only as a gift."[7]

Removing the Blocks and Barriers

Getting the soul into view is only the start. We must not mistake a glimpse as being the equivalent of fullness. Henri Nouwen tells us:

> When Anthony heard the world of Jesus, "Go and sell what you own and give the money to the poor. . . . then come and follow me," he took it as a call to escape from the compulsions of the world. He moved away from his family, lived in poverty in a hut on the edge of his village, and occupied himself with manual work and prayer. But soon he realized that more was required of him. He had to face his enemies—anger and greed—head-on and let himself be totally transformed into a new being. His old, false self had to die and a new self had to be born. For this Anthony withdrew into the complete solitude of the desert.
>
> Solitude is the furnace of transformation. Without solitude we remain victims of our society and continue to be entangled in the illusions of the false self. Jesus himself entered into this furnace.[8]

We do well to note that the Eastern Orthodox Church, which puts great emphasis on the life, doesn't offer much guidance on prayer techniques. In contrast, prayer manuals are filled with direction on one's moral posture and the necessary spiritual conditions for effective praying. *Getting right* is more important than *doing it right*.

Once we begin to develop a sense of inner space and living prayer, we will become aware of more serious barriers than simple everyday distractions. The soul is often calloused, encased, and encrusted with a protective shell.

Often considerable time is required to become aware of the barricades that years of painful experience have erected. We may not be aware that we are our own worst enemy.

Once we begin to tear away the false self, we will not find that the path is automatically easier. To the contrary, we will find ourselves in another form of spiritual warfare. We have to struggle with formerly nonthreatening demons that cohabited with us. Now the house must be cleaned and the intruders cast out. Abba Elias, one of the Desert Fathers, reminds us of where our strength must be found for this battle in the desert of our own souls.

> An old man was living in a temple and the demons came to say to him, "leave this place which belongs to us," and the old man said, "No place belongs to you." Then they began to scatter his palm leaves about, one by one, and the old man went on gathering them together with persistence. A little later the devil took his hand and pulled him to the door. When the old man reached the door, he seized the lintel with the other hand crying out, "Jesus, save me." Immediately the devil fled away. Then the old man began to weep. Then the Lord said to him, "Why are you weeping?" and the old man said, "Because the devils have dared to seize a man and treat him like this." The Lord said to him, "You had been careless. As soon as you turned to me again, you see I was beside you."[9]

Each of us must be prepared for the battle to take many forms as we push on to recover our souls fully. We must remember the one we seek is already there waiting to help us get through the blockades and the mine fields secretly set to stop us. In the silence and solitude, we must fervently seek the intervention of Christ to accomplish for us what we cannot achieve for ourselves.

Hearing His Voice

In the beginning, God speaks and everything comes into existence. In A.D. 1, God spoke again and the Word became flesh. The Creator is a God who communicates, and the recovery of the soul is the restoration of our ability to hear. Finding our soul is more than developing awareness. We are called on to a relationship analogous to what Adam and Eve knew in the Garden.

You can develop the capacity to hear your heavenly Father speak your name.

Your soul is the place of reception. David Watson put the promise in these terms. "God did not finish speaking to us when the scriptures were completed. . . . God is the living God, the God of today; and every day he wants us to enjoy a living relationship with him, involving a two-way conversation."[10]

After weeks of exploring silence and praying the Jesus Prayer, I reached the level where I was praying for an hour a day in contemplation. The experience was rich, rewarding, and reconstituting. Then one day, I realized I had reached a new plateau. Something more was just on the other side of that single hour.

At the end of one of these periods, the story of the boy Samuel's call from God came to mind. I remember Samuel wasn't clear about how God spoke. The old high priest Eli told the boy to respond to his next visitation, "Speak Lord, for your servant hears." With that phrase ringing in my mind, at the end of the next hour of silent prayer I said the same words aloud. Much to my surprise, I found my mind was filled with a new vivid dialogue.

Like a stream of consciousness, a flow of verbal direction ran through my thinking. I immediately grabbed my pencil and wrote furiously. Trying to keep from censoring myself, I simply let come what may. Eventually the words ebbed away, and I had a page full of notes.

In the following days, I eagerly pursued my newfound discipline. The flow of material increased as did my capacity to hear the voice of God. In addition, I found the direction I received was extremely helpful in making decisions and knowing the will of God. Often the communiques had messages or insights for other people. Sometimes Jesus seemed to speak as a friend. At other times, the voice seemed to be more clearly like the gentle moving of the Holy Spirit. On occasion, the majestic voice of the Father broke through. There was no question in my mind that I had found a new and profound sense of connecting with the Holy Trinity.

Slowly, I began to evolve a new sense of how the soul works. As the mind has an intuitive function, the soul has a unique sense of knowing. The more I reflected on how intuition operates, the more clear I became about my spiritual experiences.

The mind can calculate like an adding machine compiles numbers and then comes to a total, a conclusion. We call this capacity syllogistic logic. Conclusions are drawn from the sum total of our experience. On the other hand, intuition bubbles up with a logic born out of knowing. Insight offers us answers without reference to the system of compilation. We intuitively know when our children are lying or when something bad is about to happen. A message comes out of the wild blue yonder and flashes thought our minds. We know that we know.

The more I paid attention to my intuitions, the more I was aware of how God speaks in the soul. While inspiration is not nonrational or irrational, it is often beyond logic and arises, as does insight, from our inner core. We must learn neither to ignore nor to censor what bubbles up from the inner aquifers. In the beginning, the important thing is just to clear out the wellsprings for a continuous flow of inspiration.

As my collection of notes piled up, I realized that a considerable amount of material was accumulating. Some of the recordings seemed mediocre; others seemed to contain highly significant direction too important to be lost. I recognized a need to systematize my most helpful discoveries and began transferring this data into a journal.

The journal was arranged with three sections. In the first of the notebook, I kept my discoveries about prayer. I kept insights into how to pray and be spiritually aware by date. Writing Hebrew style, I recorded the promises of the Holy Spirit in the back of the book. I dated each indication of direction.

Possibly the most important section of the journal was in the middle. When I heard wrong or the promises turned out to be bogus, I recorded my error. Periodically, I would go back and try to sort out why I heard wrong. Quickly, I found the miscommunications offered very important insight into the soul as well.

Fine-tuning the Soul

Being in touch with the soul doesn't make us automatically right or every intuitive nudge correct. In fact, with time I discovered hearing God accurately, consistently, and with understanding was much more complex than I thought in the early euphoric days of spiritual breakthrough. For example, if the moral climate isn't right, the message can be distorted like sounds fading when batteries are going dead on a dictation device. Often there is considerable contamination as personal desires sweep in and pollute the message. We do well to be highly suspicious of ourselves.

How do we avoid such pitfalls? The discipline of journaling is a necessity. We have to pay the price of hours spent in intercession, meditation, and silence learning the pathways through our soul. You don't have time to do this amount of soul inquiry? Do you have time for anything else . . . lest you gain the world and lose your soul?

Many sincere people confuse their thoughts with inspiration. Whatever blips through their minds during prayer is assumed to be holy. They may start speaking aloud a prayer message to a group of listeners, but their revelation is a spiritual stream of consciousness that is nothing more than if they were talking to themselves with their eyes closed.

We need to have clear guidelines to test what is coming from the soul. Here are time-tried directions for clear reception and understanding the soul.

Soul Talk

• *Does the message square with Scripture?*
God speaks with one voice and the centuries don't change the message. Healthy people will keep referencing biblical guidelines. Compromise on this front is deadly.

• *Does the message find resonance with other spiritual people?*

We need spiritual companions in this walk. A spiritual director is a must. Sharing the inner movements of the soul helps establish a vital objectivity that distances us from the false self. If we are uncomfortable sharing some message or aspect of the soul with confidential friends, we have a strong clue something is wrong.

• *Do we need a competent therapist for some issues?*

The emphasis is on *competent*. Wounds from childhood and traumas along the way seriously damage many of us and make it much more difficult to get in touch with the soul. These same conflicts distort inspiration. Therapy may be a necessity.

• *Does it stand the test of time?*

God is consistent with himself, and subsequently truth is one of the best indicators of what he is saying. Like the sun coming up, the truth will get brighter with the passing of time. Check your journal periodically to see if verifications are there.

• *Is the emotional tone spiritually significant?*

Often people are told, "You will know the will of God because of the peace you have." Half truth! In many instances the Holy Spirit challenges, corrects, and doesn't make us happy. As a matter of fact I am suspicious of inspiration that only confirms my prejudgments. When a contrary or surprising emotion appears, I take the uncomfortable feeling very seriously.

• *What fruit does this spiritual encounter produce?*

Am I becoming more gentle, loving, thoughtful, preserving? Is the work of the Kingdom being accomplished through my spiritual discoveries? If the answers aren't positive, I need to take a second look.

These guidelines will help you tune out static and distortion. And remember, the more you listen, the greater will become your awareness of your soul.

Finding a Companion for the Journey

Prolonged time with the soul often reveals we have significant issues that need someone else's insight. Possibly we need spiritual healing. Often, we must find spiritual companions trained as doctors of the soul. A competent spiritual director with the capacity to be a soulmate is a rare and invaluable friend.

Long a discipline in the Roman Catholic, Orthodox, and Anglican traditions, spiritual directors are trained to blend scripture, psychology, and theology in the art of restoring souls. Expert listeners, spiritual directors probe the soul, removing emotional shrapnel and splinters from bad memories, and unmasking the blind spots in our perceptions of ourselves. They help us sort out confusion and shame so that the secret self can emerge and be examined.

A spiritual director is essential to test what we believe the Holy Spirit is saying. Self-deception is an inevitable part of every life. A straightforward spiritual friend unafraid to tell the truth will keep us from the seductiveness of our dreams and the nonsense of our fantasies.

Today confusion of the soul abounds! A few decades ago, no one dared to baptize their opinions by saying, "The Lord told me." Today every impulse and whim of the faithful seems to be completely God-breathed. Rather than saying, "I am moving to another church because I like the other place better," everyone is now "led to a new ministry." Many Christians would be saved considerable embarrassment by having a spiritual director help them sort out the baloney from the blessing.

If nothing else, a spiritual director will help us maintain the disciplines necessary to consistent living out of the soul.

Finding Our Way Home

What does it mean to have found your soul? Not as an idea but as an inner reality? Not only is God-consciousness recovered but a profound sense of relationship with the Ultimate Lover of our soul follows.

This is the nature of the encounter, not that I am stumbling towards the Abba Father, but that the Abba Father is running towards me. It is not that I love God but that God believes in me. The discovery at the heart of contemplation is not that I am contemplating the divine love, but that the divine love is contemplating me. He sees me and understands and accepts me, he has compassion on me, he creates me afresh from moment to moment, and he protects me and is with me through death and into life beyond.[11]

Chapter 13

LIVING
IN THE
SOUL

O nce the renowned philosopher Arthur Schopenhauer was walking obliviously down the
street in deep thought when he accidentally ran into a
stranger. Schopenhauer's seeming indifference caused the
other man to shout angrily, "Just who do you think
you are?"

The dismayed thinker looked at the upset pedestrian and
replied in consternation, "Who am I? How I wish I knew!"

Even if apocryphal, the incident is a good parable of
the twentieth century. Leonard Bernstein observed, "Half
the people are drowned and the other half are swimming
in the wrong direction."[1] Even though decades ago, T. S.
Eliot warned us about becoming hollow people with
straw-stuffed heads, we are often gleefully unaware of our
deadly predicament. Technology saves us from confrontation with harsh reality by offering an infinite number of
new toys each year that keep us from recognizing our
aimless meandering trek from birth to the grave. No time

left to think while the menu options of the Internet are popping up before our eyes. Just push the buttons and bring up the endless choices! Are these diversions any different from offering lollipops to an upset child as a distraction from the pain?

In *The Sane Society,* psychologist Erich Fromm gave us the bottom line: "In the nineteenth century the problem was that God is dead; in the twentieth century the problem is that man is dead."[2]

Our Hope

The answer is not religion per se. Unfortunately, soulless churches have often promised peace at any price, offering sterile placebos for cancer of the soul. Emotional tranquility is the prize regardless of what must be denied. God is a celestial Tylenol painkiller to be taken every morning and night until we no longer feel what we are sure we feel.

An unknown author wrote, "For some people religion is like an artificial limb. It has neither warmth nor life; and although it helps them to stumble along, it never becomes part of them. It must be strapped on each day."[3]

The new phenomena of the 1990s are self-invented, do-it-yourself religions using Christian language but with no connection to the church or its past. Often called New Age, these groups talk about spirituality but can't offer transcendence. They wade into the marketplace selling emotional well-being by teaching how to think more positively or rely on psychic powers. However, prayer in this context is essentially nothing more than talking to oneself. Talk of soul is more on the level of Ray Charles belting out inner agony. The New Agers, too, are specialists in crutches, artificial legs, and plastic arms.

In the past twelve chapters, a better alternative has been advanced. Our hope is the recovery of the soul.

Scripture tells us no matter how emaciated and abused, the soul can be found and restored. The four Gospels demand we stop in our tracks, turn around, and start traveling toward God. During the journey, our souls will be restored. In a few sweeping sentences, Jesus taught us what it means to give up mindless distractions as well as our quixotic quest for fame, fortune, and significance in order to become whole. "Therefore I tell you, do not be anxious about your life, what you shall eat or what you shall drink, nor about your body, what you shall put on. And which of you by being anxious can add one cubit to his span of life? But seek first his kingdom and his righteousness, and all these things shall be yours as well."[4]

Life in the Kingdom restores the soul and our identity.

The framers of the Westminster Catechism had this objective when they suggested the purpose of life is to know and enjoy God forever. The point of our existence is not to do or accomplish any particular thing. Rather, the restoration of spiritual relationship is the singular most significant achievement of anyone's lifetime.

Such a lofty goal is achievable only when our sails are set not only to find the soul but to live in that land.

Our Common Destiny

From the beginning of this book, we have been faced with a problem. We are looking for something no one has ever seen. Jesus had the same difficulty in calling people to life. In Carson McCullers's novel *The Heart Is a Lonely Hunter,* a teenager tries to explain to a deaf mute how music sounds. With frantic gestures, the girl stands in front of poor Mr.

Singer trying to get him to read her lips. Eventually she realizes how hopeless her attempts are. One can't explain color to the blind or sound to the deaf—or life to the dead.

Our task in the previous pages has not been easier. And yet we have seen a multitude of witnesses from across the centuries point the way. They told us the soul is not a place as much as a capacity. As important as is the reestablishment of contact, the real objective is a life of continuous dialogue.

Few people understood living out of the soul as well as did the Quaker theologian Thomas Kelly.

> Deep within us all there is an amazing inner sanctuary of the soul, a holy place, a Divine Center, a speaking Voice, to which we may continuously return. Eternity is at our hearts, pressing upon our time-torn lives, warming us with intimations of an astounding destiny, calling us home unto Itself. Yielding to these persuasions, gladly committing ourselves in body and soul, utterly and completely, to the Light Within which illumines the face of God and casts new shadows and new glories upon the face of men. It is a seed stirring to life if we do not choke it. It is the Shekinah of the soul, the Presence in the midst. Here is the Slumbering Christ, stirring to be awakened, to become the soul we clothe in earthly form and action.[5]

Our task is to keep one foot in the world of bills, babies, and doorbells while keeping the other in the hidden place of eternity. Our vision must constantly shift back and forth from this realm of artificial lightbulbs to the place where the glorious light of God alone shines. Once we've found focus, we must make sure our visits are far more than seasonal or prompted by the pressure of problems or personal tragedy. Destiny is not "doing something" but living there.

The Answer

Once the Holy Spirit restores the soul, we discover the risen Christ calls us by name as surely as He summoned Mary of Magdela on the first Easter morning. Individual and unique ways of hearing the gentle calling of God become very important. Our task is to live at the place where the voice arises.

The objective of our spiritual quest is not to collect right ideas, perfect our theology, find ecstatic religious experiences, seek the latest avant-garde fad, or even learn new rules to live by. The goal is to live out of our soul minute by minute, hour by hour, day by day.

John Woolman, the Quaker tailor, attempted to arrange every aspect of his private and business life so nothing could crowd out his continuous inner experience of Christ. As he worked from the altar of his soul, Woolman was also increasingly aware of the evils of his day: slave trading, usury, and the Indian wars.

Thomas Kelly described the practice of believers like Woolman in these terms: "There is a way of ordering our mental life on more than one level at once. On one level we may be thinking, discussing, seeing, calculating, meeting all the demands of external affairs. But deep within, behind the scenes, at a profounder level, we may also be in prayer and adoration, song and worship and a gentle receptiveness to divine breathings."[6]

Kelly believed that living in the soul means constantly bringing all the affairs of life into the Presence and rethinking each event in the Light of the Christ before bringing it back into the world of daily events. He said perceptively, "Facts remain fact, when brought into the Presence in the deeper level, but their value, their significance, is wholly realigned."[7]

Living from the soul is quite practical. Henry Blackaby and Claude King described the straightforward nature of soul-centered life in their book, *Experiencing God*.

> God is absolutely trustworthy. You can trust Him to guide you and provide for you. Remember: "It is God who works in you both to will and to do for His good pleasure" (Phil. 2:13). Would you consider doing the following?
>
> - Agree with God that you will follow Him one day at a time.
> - Agree to follow Him even when He does not spell out all the details.
> - Agree that you will let Him be your Way.
>
> Now consider praying this prayer: Lord, I will do anything that your kingdom requires of me. Wherever you want me to be, I'll go. Whatever the circumstances, I'm willing to follow. If you want to meet a need through my life, I am your servant; and I will do whatever is required.[8]

How Shall We Hear?

The last chapter encouraged you to develop the discipline of listening as you quietly wait at the center of your soul. Sacred history demonstrates the Holy Spirit communicates with us in many ways. For many, the Scripture is the place of direct speech. The more time spent in the Word, the clearer the directives become.

Other Christians find Holy Communion to be their primary means of encounter. Wine and bread are visible signs of an invisible transaction with the soul. As food nourishes the body, the sacrament feeds the soul.

Quakers sit in silence and wait. The Orthodox use icons, holy pictures, to experience God. Pentecostals speak in tongues and listen for prophecies and exhortations to find God. Christians have used a wide range of prayer methods to help believers dwell in the place of the inner light. The most important issue is that we *live in this* place of encounter.

How does the unseen encounter happen? Citizens of this age of technology should have few problems in accepting invisible communication. We are immersed in and totally depend on unseen forms of messages. From birth onward, we live with the knowledge that unobservable pictures, music, sounds, and speech are floating through our homes. At the flip of a switch, stereo and television sets translate invisible radio frequencies into sitcoms and concerts. On a far more sophisticated level, the divine receiver in our soul tunes in spiritual dimensions too refined for any spectrograph to detect.

Forget the E-mail, the fax, and the latest improvements on your computer's modem for a while. Let soul communication rebuild your life through eternal communiques.

Dwell in the Silence

We have already discovered the necessity of solitude. Life in the soul demands further exploration of silence. No easy task for a generation trained to turn on the TV, radio, and stereo full blast as soon as we hit an empty house.

Conditioned to drown out our loneliness, we fear being alone. Ironically, the clatter only increases the problem.

Thomas Merton observed:

Ours is a time of anxiety because we have willed it to be so. Our anxiety is not imposed on us by force from outside. We impose it on our world and upon one another from within ourselves. Sanctity in such an age means, no doubt, traveling from the area of anxiety to the area in which there is no anxiety or perhaps it may mean learning from God, to be without anxiety in the midst of anxiety. Fundamentally, as Max Picard points out, it probably comes to this: living in a silence which so reconciles the contradictions within us that, although they remain within us, they cease to be a problem. Contradictions have always existed in the soul of man. But it is only when we prefer analysis to silence that they become a constant and insoluble problem. We are not meant to resolve all contradictions but to live with them and rise above them and see them in the light of exterior and objective values which make them trivial by comparison. Silence, then, belongs to the substance of sanctity.[9]

The soul must be cultivated in the face of the inescapable consternation and dread with which we live. Silence becomes a place of transformation rather than escape.

The longer we practice walking through the silence, the more skilled we become at quickly finding the serene center. In this holy place, we grow into what Paul called, "the fullness of the stature of Jesus Christ." Our age has filled its quota of spiritual pygmies and spiritual retards. The time is at hand for a new race of spiritual giants to appear. They will be born out of silence.

In time, we will learn how to carry the silence with us even into the busy world of noise and distraction. Practicing aloneness equips us to keep the center of our soul protected from a stampede of the herd. Thomas Kelly learned the secret well.

How, then shall we lay hold of that Life and Power, and live the life of prayer without ceasing? By quiet, persistent practice in turning of all our being, day and night, in prayer and inward worship and surrender toward Him who calls in the deeps of our soul. Mental habits of inward orientation must be established. An inner, secret turning to God can be made fairly steady, after weeks and months and years of practice and lapses and failures and returns. Begin now, as you read these words, as you sit in your chair, to offer your whole selves, utterly and in joyful abandon, in quiet, glad surrender to Him who is within. In secret ejaculations of praise, turn in humble wonder to the Light, faint though it may be. Keep contact with the world of sense and meanings. Here is no discipline in absent-mindedness. Walk and talk and work and laugh with your friends. But behind the scenes, keep the life of simple prayer and inward worship. Keep it up throughout the day. Let inward prayer be your last act before you fall asleep and the first act when you awake. And in time you will find as did Brother Lawrence, that "those who have the gale of the Holy Spirit go forward even in sleep."[10]

The Cloister of the Heart

Because Jesus Christ is the same yesterday, today, and forever, He alone is the final guide and goal. Far from a figure in the past, the risen Christ stands on the other side of silence waiting to restore us to himself.

Many church people are surprised to hear that communication is reciprocal. They hope their intercessions will get beyond the roof but know nothing of anything coming back down. Because contemporary Christians tend toward a "fast good" approach to prayer, spiritual malnutrition is rampant. We grab "a little something" to keep us going as we hurry on to the next event in our lives.

Only by living in the quiet center of the soul can we learn to listen. Through contemplation we learn to let the speech of God come up from our souls. We must build on the basic disciplines discussed in the last chapter. Thomas Kelly understood this deeper level well.

> There is no new technique for entrance upon this stage where the soul in its deeper levels is continuously at Home in Him. The processes of inward prayer do not grow more complex, but more simple. In the early weeks we begin with simple, whispered words. Formulate them spontaneously, "Thine only. Thine only." Or seize upon a fragment of the Psalms: "so panteth my soul after Thee, O God." Repeat them inwardly, over and over again. For the conscious cooperation of the surface level is needed at first, before prayer sinks into the second level as habitual divine orientation. Change the phrases, as you feel led, from hour to hour or from forenoon to afternoon. If you wander, return and begin again. But the time will come when verbalization is not so imperative, and yields place to the attitudes of soul which you meant the words to express, attitudes of humble bowing before Him, attitudes of lifting high your whole being before Him that the Light may shine into the last crevice and

drive away all darkness, attitudes of approach and nestling in the covert of His wings, attitudes of amazement and marvel at His transcendent glory, attitudes of self-abandonment, attitudes of feeding in an inward Holy Supper upon the Bread of Life.[11]

Just to know Him is enough to make any difficulty in the journey meaningless.

The Conditions for Abiding

Jesus said, "If a person loves me, he will keep my word. And my Father will love him and we will come to him and make our home with him."[12] The critical principle for living in the soul is obedience. We need not be theologians, mystics, prophets, or hermits to abide constantly at the center. The old hymn was clear: "Trust and obey for there's no other way to be happy in Jesus."

St. Augustine offered the simple principle, *credo un intelligum*. Reversing the usual procedure by which people determine what is true through empirical evidence, Augustine proclaimed, "I believe and therefore I know." Through and by obedience, we authenticate and verify the truth of our faith. Spiritual knowledge and reality is not the result of what can be proved. Only by living out what we believe day by day, year by year, do we come in time to know that our convictions are more real than the tangible world around us.

Simple faithfulness is a form of living out of the soul. Like the use of memory or retaining muscle tone, use is critical to maintenance. Daily obedience is the equivalent of a trip to the gym to keep the body toned.

In *Experiencing God,* obedience is described as our moment of truth:

> In many ways, obedience is your moment of truth.
> What you *do* will:
> 1. Reveal what you believe about Him.
> 2. Determine whether you will experience His mighty work in you and through you.
> 3. Determine whether you will come to know Him more intimately.[13]

"Whenever you sense that obedience is too costly, it indicates that you have misunderstood who you are and what you have."[14]

Like trust in a marriage relationship, faithfulness is essential if we are to live in the soul with the One who is the lover of our soul. Fidelity is the secret of spiritual knowledge.

The Shape of Eternity in Us

We can put away the anatomy charts and X-ray machines. The soul will not be located with a stethoscope or electrodes. Poets and artists are better guides than anthropologists and scientists. The poor in spirit will get there much quicker than the brilliant and forceful. Rather than peering through a microscope, we do better to get down on our knees.

The longer we live in our souls, the more obviously will be the imprint of eternity on our lives.

Irenaeus once said of Jesus the Christ's restoration of our souls, "He became what we are that we might become who He is." The Bible speaks of this final singleness as soul. The soul is the real us, our essence, the fingerprint of God on our lives. Once renewed, our soul is both the center and circumference of our existence.

What might such life in the soul look like? Consider two concluding parables.

Remember the story of the leper on Umbrian Plain?

One day Francis of Assisi was riding across the fields on his way home when he came upon a hideous beggar by the roadside. No disease put greater fear in human hearts than the one that covered the body with flesh-eating sores. Conquering his own fear, Francis stopped and put a coin in the hand of the broken man. Suddenly seized by an inspiration of love beyond himself, Francis bent down and gave the man a kiss of peace on the lips. Deep within the soul of Francis, new life stirred and a new life was begun.

Of this moment, Francis wrote in his diary, "The Lord Himself led me amongst them, and I showed mercy to them, and what I left them, what had seemed bitter to me was changed into sweetness of body and soul."[15]

The rest of the legend tells us that as Francis rode away, he looked back only to discover no one was there. Instantly he realized he had kissed the Lord. Such is life in the soul.

Or do you know the story of the Curé d'Ars?

As a young man, he was considered something of a dunce. He further embarrassed his parents by deciding to become a priest. In his first parish assignment, the vicar considered the recent seminarian too stupid to preach Sunday sermons. But when the bishop gave the devout young man his own parish, his meager gifts were completely offered to God. Rather than rely on scholarship, personality, or public relations skills, the priest completely gave his soul to God in fervent daily prayer.

From his obscure post, the Curé's fame began to spread across France. Hundreds of thousands of people began making pilgrimages to Ars to sit at his feet and be blessed by the simple priest's teaching and preaching. When he would leave the church after a service, the pressure of the crowds was so great, thirty minutes would be required to cross the small square in front of the church.

Sixty-six years after his death, the Curé d'Ars was canonized as the saint of parish priests in 1925. Because he gave of his humble gifts in faithful obedience, the Curé's soul was a marvel to behold.[16]

Notes

CHAPTER ONE

1. Richards, *Centering,* 33.

CHAPTER FOUR

1. "Tough Talk on Entertainment," 32.
2. Ibid., 33.
3. Ibid., 34.

CHAPTER SIX

1. Keen, *Fire in the Belly,* 110–11.
2. Daniel 2:27–28.
3. Psalms 26:1–3; 102:1–4.
4. Marcus, *Mystery Train,* 32–36.
5. Burns, *The Late Liz,* 1.
6. Ibid., 342.

CHAPTER SEVEN

1. Styron, *Sophie's Choice,* 177.
2. Wiesel, *Night,* 109.
3. ten Boom, *Hiding Place,* 198–99.

CHAPTER EIGHT

1. The previous chapter raised the question of the different ways Christians viewed where the soul was between the moment of death and the Great Resurrection. Tertullian's writing reflects one position the early church took. In his writing, Hades does not mean what the contemporary Christian means by hell. Hell is final punishment.

In addition, this discussion of an intermediate state should not be confused with the medieval idea of purgatory to be developed later. The issue for Tertullian was earning not salvation but ultimate perfection.

CHAPTER TWELVE

1. Nouwen, *The Way of the Heart*, 59.
2. Bloom, *Courage to Pray*, 41.
3. *Reflections of the Jesus Prayer*, 21.
4. Ibid., 25.
5. Ibid., 25.
6. *The Cloud of Unknowing*, 51.
7. Merton, *Contemplative Prayer*, 115.
8. Nouwen, *The Way of the Heart*, 25.
9. Ward, *The Sayings of the Desert Fathers*, 69.
10. Watson, *Discipleship*, 149.
11. Verney, *Into the New Age*, 91–92.

CHAPTER THIRTEEN

1. Link, *Take Off Your Shoes*, 20.
2. Ibid., 12.
3. Ibid., 42.
4. Matthew 6:25–33.

5. Kelly, *A Testament of Devotion*, 29.
6. Ibid., 35.
7. Ibid., 36.
8. Blackaby and King, *Experiencing God*, 23.
9. Merton, *Thoughts on Solitude*, 82–83.
10. Kelly, *A Testament of Devotion*, 38–39.
11. Ibid., 43.
12. John 14:23.
13. Blackaby and King, *Experiencing God*, 157.
14. Ibid., 165.
15. Paton, *Instrument of Thy Peace*.
16. Ibid., 104.

Bibliography

Andrews, Robert. *The Concise Columbia Dictionary of Quotations.* New York: AVM Books, 1989.

Barrett, William. *Death of the Soul: From Descartes to the Computer.* Garden City, N.Y.: Anchor/Doubleday, 1986.

Bennett, William J. "America, What's Gone Wrong?" *Current Thoughts and Trends,* July 1994, Vol. 10, No. 7, 24.

_____. "A Nation's Spiritual Decay," Sower (Spring 1994): 10.

Berg, Elizabeth. "What's Your Hurry?" *Readers Digest,* September 1993, 19.

Berman, Phillip L. *The Search for Meaning.* New York: Ballantine, 1990.

Blackaby, Henry T., and Claude V. King. *Experiencing God.* Nashville: Broadman & Holman, 1994.

Blanchard, John, comp. *More Gathered Gold: A Treasury of Quotations for Christians.* Hertfordshire, England: Evangelical, 1986.

Bloom, Anthony. *Courage to Pray.* New York: Paulist Press, 1973.

Bly, Robert, trans. *Times Alone: Selected Poems of Antonio Machado.* Wesleyan University Press, 1983.

ten Boom, Corrie. *The Hiding Place.* Washington Depot, Conn.: Chosen Books, 1971.

Bowles, Linda. "Battle Rages Over America's Soul," *Daily Oklahoman,* August 10, 1994.

Boyd, Jeffrey H. *Affirming the Soul: Remarkable Conversations Between Mental Health Professionals and an Ordained Minister.* Cheshire, Conn.: Soul Research Institute, 1994.

Brown, Colin, ed. *The New International Dictionary of New Testament Theology.* Grand Rapids, Mich.: Zondervan, 1975.

Burns, Elizabeth. *The Late Liz.* New York: Meredith, 1957.

Canfield, Jack, and Mark Victor Hansen. *A Second Helping of Chicken Soup for the Soul: 101 More Stories to Open the Heart and Rekindle the Spirity.* Deerfield Beach, Fla.: Health Communications, 1995.

Carver, Raymond. "Meditation on a Line from Saint Teresa." *No Heroics Please: Raymond Carver Uncollected Writings.* New York: Vantage, 1992.

The Cloud of Unknowing. New York: Penguin, 1977.

Coles, Robert. *The Spiritual Life of Children.* Houghton Mifflin, 1990.

Corbiere, Edouard. *The Slave Trader.* New York: Harry N. Abrams, 1992.

Cousineau, Phil. *Soul: An Archaeology.* San Francisco: HarperSan Francisco, 1994.

Cousins, Norman. *The Celebration of Life: A Dialogue on Hope, Spirit, and the Immortality of the Soul.* New York: Bantam, 1991.

Doan, Eleanor. *Speakers Sourcebook II.* Grand Rapids, Mich.: Zondervan, 1968.

Doyle, Brendan, ed. *Meditations with Julian of Norwich.* Santa Fe: Bear & Company, 1983.

Eliade, Mircea, "The Immortality of the Soul." In *No Souvenirs.* Translated by Fred H. Johnson, Jr. Harper & Row. 1977.

Farrell, Frank, *Tabletalk.* June 1992.

Feder, Don. *A Jewish Conservative Looks at Pagan America.* Lafayette, La.: Huntington House, 1993.

Ferguson. Sheila. *Soul Food.* Grove Press, 1989.

Fitzgerald, F. Scott, and Edmund Wilson, eds. *The Crackup.* New York: New Directions in Publishing Corp., 1993.

Fox, Matthew. *Meditations with Meister Eckhart.* Santa Fe: Bear & Company, 1983.

French, R. M., trans. *The Way of a Pilgrim.* San Francisco: HarperSanFrancisco, 1991.

Friedrich, Gerhard, ed. *Theological Dictionary of the New Testament.* Grand Rapids, Mich.: Wm. B. Eerdmans, 1974.

Gallup, George. "A Nation in Recovery," *Emerging Trends* 16, no. 10, December 1994, 1–2.

Gordon, Arthur. "Six Minutes of Awe," *Guideposts,* January 1992, 13.

Greil, Marcus. *Mystery Train.* New York: Dutton, a division of Penguin USA, 1990.

Guralnick, Peter. *Sweet Soul Music: Rhythm and Blues and the Southern Dream of Freedom.* New York: Harper & Row, 1986.

Hale, Sue. "Collective Soul on the Mend," *Sunday Oklahoman,* 30 April 1995.

Hammerschlag, Carl A. *The Theft of the Spirit: A Journey to Spiritual Healing with Native Americans.* New York: Simon & Schuster, 1993.

Harvey, Paul. "It's Time for Americans to Return to Their Homes." *Daily Oklahoman,* 28 March 1994.

Hawthorne, Gerald F., and Ralph P. Martin, eds. *Dictionary of Paul and His Letters.* Downers Grove, Ill.: InterVarsity, 1993.

Herbert, Bob. "A Reckless Journey." *Black Chronicle,* 5 January 1995, A-5.

Jones, Timothy. "Penchant for the Paranormal." *Leadership* 16, no. 1 (Winter 1994).

Keen, Sam. *Fire in the Belly.*

Kelly, Thomas R. *A Testament of Devotion.* New York: Harper & Brothers, 1941.

à Kempis, Thomas. *The Imitation of Christ.* Nashville: Thomas Nelson, 1979.

Lacayo, Richard. "Are Music and Movies Killing America's Soul?" *Time,* 12 June 1995, 24–30.

Landers, Ann. Column. *Saturday Oklahoman and Times,* 25 December 1993.

_____. "The Saturday Review Youthworker Update." November 1994.

Link, Mark, S. J. *He Is the Still Point of the Turning World*. Chicago: Argus Communications, 1971.

———. *Take Off Your Shoes*. Chicago: Argus Communications, 1971.

Mead, Frank S., ed. *The Encyclopedia of Religious Quotations*. Westwood, N.J.: Fleming H. Revell. 1965.

Meditations with Hildegard of Bingen. Versions by Gabriele Uhlein. Santa Fe: Bear & Company, 1982.

Merton, Thomas. *Contemplative Prayer* New York: Farrar, Straus and Giroux, 1973.

———. *Thoughts in Solitude*.

Morrison, James D., ed. *Masterpieces of Religious Verse*. New York: Harper and Bros., 1948.

Needleman, Jacob. *Lost Christianity*. New York: Element Books, 1993.

Noffke, Suzanne, O. P., trans. *Catherine of Siena: The Dialogue*. New York: Paulist Press, 1980.

Nouwen, Henri J. M. *The Way of the Heart*. New York: Seabury, 1981.

Paton, Alan. *Instrument of Thy Peace: The Prayer of St. Francis*. New York: Seabury, 1968.

Pentz, Croft M. *The Complete Book of Zingers*. Wheaton, Ill.: Tyndale House, 1990.

Pepper, Margaret, comp. *The Harper Religious and Inspirational Quotation Companion*. New York: Harper & Row, 1989.

Pope John XXIII. *Journal of a Soul*. New York: McGraw-Hill, 1965.

Quoist, Michel. *Prayers*. New York: Sheed & Ward, 1963.

Raines, Robert A. *Creative Brooding*. New York: Macmillan, 1966.

———. *Soundings*. New York: Harper & Row, 1970.

Rainie, Harrison. "The Buried Sounds of Children Crying." *U.S. News & World Report,* 1 May 1995, 10.

Raspberry, William. "We Must Learn Why We Are Producing Such Violent People." *Dallas Morning News,* 23 August 1993, 13A.

Reflections of the Jesus Prayer. Denville, N.J.: Dimension, 1948.

Richards, Mary Caroline. *Centering*. Middletown, Conn.: Wesleyan University Press, 1962.

Roberts, Alexander, and James Donaldson, eds. *The Ante-Nicene Fathers: Translations of the Writings of the Fathers Down to A.D. 325*. Grand Rapids, Mich.: Wm. B. Eerdmans, 1989.

Rosenthal, Marvin J. "America's Meteoric Descent into Darkness," *Pulpit Helps,* August 1994, 24.

Saint Teresa of Avila. *The Interior Castle*. Translated and edited by E. Allison Peers. New York: Image, 1961.

Sardello, Robert, "Facing the World with Soul." In *Facing the World with Soul*. Hudson, N.Y.: Lindisfarne, 1991.

Schaff, Philip, ed. *A Select Library of the Nicene and Post-Nicene Fathers of the Christian Church*. Grand Rapids: Wm. B. Eerdmans.

Sheen, Fulton, J. *Life of Christ*. Garden City, N.Y.: Image, 1977.

Simpson, James B., comp. *Simpson's Contemporary Quotations*. Boston: Houghton Mifflin, 1988.

Simsic, Wayne. *Praying with John of the Cross*. Winona, Minn.: Christian Brothers, 1993.

Singer, June. *Boundaries of the Soul: The Practice of Jung's Psychology*. Garden City, N.Y.: Doubleday, 1972.

Steiner, Rudolf. "The Two Streams of Soul." *Metamorphoses of the Soul,* vol. 2. Translated by C. Davy and C. mon Arnim. Anthroposophic Press, 1990.

Styron, William. *Sophie's Choice*. New York: Bantam Books, 1979.

Swindoll, Charles. *Stress Fractures*. Grand Rapids, Mich.: Zondervan, 1990.

Thompson, Francis, "The Hound of Heaven." *Masterpieces of Religious Verse*. New York: Harper & Brothers, 1948.

Todd, Loretto. *Tortoise the Trickster and Other Folktales from Cameroon*. Philadelphia: Benjamins North America, 1982.

Tripp, Rhoda Thomas, comp. *The International Thesaurus of Quotations*. New York: Harper & Row, 1970.

Underhill, Evelyn. *Mysticism*. Cleveland and New York: World Publishing, 1970.

Underwood, John. *The Boston Globe*.

Verney, Stephen. *Into the New Age*. Centerport, N.Y.: John M. Fontana Publishing, 1976.

Walker, Alice. "They Want Your Soul." In *Living by the Word: Selected Writings: 1973–1987*. New York: Harcourt, Brace & Company, 1988.

Walsh, Kenneth T. "The Soul and Character of America." *U.S. News & World Report*, 8 May 1995, 10.

Ward, Benedicta, trans. *The Sayings of the Desert Fathers*. London: Mowbrays, 1975.

Watson, David. *Discipleship*. Hodder & Stoughton, 1981.

Wells, Jr., Albert M., comp. *Inspiring Quotations: Contemporary and Classical*. Nashville: Thomas Nelson, 1988.

Wiesel, Elie. *Night*. New York: Bantam, 1960.

Wright, Robert. "The Evolution of Despair." *Time*, 28 August 1995, 50.